U-Turn
Teaching

Rich Allen dedicates this book to those people who prompted the key

U-Turns that put him on his present professional path:

Linda Brown, Dave Edwards, Eric Jensen, and Don Freeman.

Jenn Currie dedicates this book . . .

To my students ~ past, present and future; you are the reason for my U-Turn.

To my mom and Dave ~ for your unconditional love, support,
and encouragement through this exciting journey.

To my husband, Scott ~ for your patience, tolerance, and understanding
as I took so much time away from 'us' to pursue this dream. I know it wasn't always
easy taking the backseat as I tap, tap, tapped away upstairs. And, ultimately, I want
to thank you for your dependable encouragement and support. You never doubted
my ability, even when I often did. For that, I am grateful.

To my dearest friends Chris Straub and Darlene Waldorf ~ your unwavering
support over the last nine years has been a HUGE contributing factor to my success.
Thank you so much for listening to my rants and raves, your shoulders to cry
on, your laughter that fills my soul, and your brilliant brains to pick.
I'm so indebted to you!

U-Turn
Teaching

Strategies to Accelerate Learning and Transform Middle School Achievement

Rich Allen
Jenn Currie

CORWIN
A SAGE Company

CORWIN
A SAGE Company

FOR INFORMATION:

Corwin
A SAGE Company
2455 Teller Road
Thousand Oaks, California 91320
(800) 233-9936
www.corwin.com

SAGE Publications Ltd.
1 Oliver's Yard
55 City Road
London EC1Y 1SP
United Kingdom

SAGE Publications India Pvt. Ltd.
B 1/I 1 Mohan Cooperative Industrial Area
Mathura Road, New Delhi 110 044
India

SAGE Publications Asia-Pacific Pte. Ltd.
3 Church Street
#10-04 Samsung Hub
Singapore 049483

Acquisitions Editor: Jessica Allan
Associate Editor: Allison Scott
Editorial Assistant: Lisa Whitney
Permissions Editor: Karen Ehrmann
Project Editor: Veronica Stapleton
Copy Editor: Diane DiMura
Typesetter: C&M Digitals (P) Ltd.
Proofreader: Dennis W. Webb
Indexer: Jean Casalegno
Cover Designer: Karine Hovsepian

Printed in the United States of America

Library of Congress Cataloging-in-Publication Data

Allen, Richard, 1957 Sept. 28- author.

U-turn teaching : strategies to accelerate learning and transform middle school achievement/Rich Allen and Jenn Currie.

pages cm
Includes bibliographical references and index.

ISBN 978-1-4129-9646-4 (pbk.)

1. Middle school education. 2. Middle school teaching. 3. Motivation in education. 4. Effective teaching. I. Currie, Jenn, author. II. Title.

LB1623.A55 2012
373.236—dc23   2012016182

This book is printed on acid-free paper.

12 13 14 15 16 10 9 8 7 6 5 4 3 2 1

Contents

Foreword

The Story of Jenn

Seven years ago, Jenn Currie—a middle school teacher of nine years—was close to burning out. Exasperated with state mandates and exhausted by unmotivated, disrespectful students, she was about to throw in the teaching towel. But then she discovered the theories behind brain-based learning and began to understand why her classroom was so chaotic and unproductive. She realized her traditional teaching strategies weren't creating conditions that help the human brain to take in, process, and remember information—in fact, the way she was teaching was sometimes actually hindering the learning process.

This revelation was the catalyst for Jenn to make a U-turn in her teaching practice. Starting from scratch, she has developed a radically different TEAM-based approach to teaching founded on Dr. Rich Allen's *Green Light* education strategies. In Jenn's new classroom format, every activity and strategy is designed to proactively support learning—and the results have been phenomenal.

Her rural, low socioeconomic, push-in classroom is now significantly outperforming all others in Grades 4–8 in her district, with students consistently scoring well above average on state assessment testing. From being a battleground, Jenn's classroom has done a complete U-turn to become a dynamic, collaborative environment where students are deeply engaged in learning while working in teams.

Moreover, Jenn's new strategies have virtually eliminated behavioral problems, enabling her to spend more time actually teaching, to the extent that she is able to complete the required state content standards ahead of schedule. Her classroom is a well-oiled machine where students *trust, encourage, accept,* and *motivate* each other to the point where **they** take responsibility for their own learning and that of others. As their teacher, Jenn's role has morphed into that of a coach—guiding and encouraging from the sidelines to strengthen the learning process.

This dramatic, cultural shift has instilled a love of learning in her students. Jenn's foundational methodology leads to student success both in and out of the classroom. Her students aren't just academic achievers; their new classroom culture turns them into self-reliant, considerate, hardworking citizens. Previously disinterested, unmotivated, and disruptive middle school students—who arrived with thick files and warnings from other teachers—now love school and are achieving beyond their and their parents' wildest dreams.

I was principal of Commodore Perry when Jennifer Currie initially began her interest and research in brain-based teaching. I witnessed Jennifer's systematic implementation of brain-based strategies, which led to outstanding student achievement. She continues to be an exemplar in the classroom and in the professional development community of the district through her reflective and innovative approaches to education.

–Pam Slatcoff, retired principal, Commodore Perry School District

Tanner transformed from a non-reader to a voracious reader, and his results began to soar. Up until Mrs. Currie's class, Tanner had always struggled academically.

–Wendy H., parent

Thank you for making me different. Thank you for making me believe in myself. You have done something nobody else could.

–Danielle, age 11

Mrs. Currie's fifth-grade classroom is the one and only year James has not had behavioral issues in school!

–Tina McCartney, Instructional Support Teacher

At the beginning of the year, most of us weren't hitting the bull's eye of success in the reading department, or certain other departments, depending on the kid. But, as the summer started to near, we were hitting the bull's eye blindfolded, all because of my fifth-grade teacher Mrs. Currie.

–Letter to the editor, Sami Armour, age 11

Thank you for all you do for your students. Kaitlyn has really enjoyed this school year with you. Plus her grades have improved, and her AR levels have doubled. We are so proud of her.

–Tracey V., parent

Finally, Jenn's teaching U-turn has reignited her love of teaching. She now positively looks forward to having *difficult* students in her class, confident that she holds the keys to unlocking their potential.

This book is designed to help other middle school teachers replicate Jenn's strategies and results in their classrooms. Jenn and Rich hope you have the courage to try something different and make a U-turn in your teaching—in the process, creating life changing moments for you and your students.

Who am I?

I am the one person who always greets them with a smile.
I am the person who cheers loudest when they succeed.
I am the person they trust to catch them when they fall.
I am the person who will not let them fail.
I am the person who believes in them.
I am . . . their teacher.

—Jenn Currie

Acknowledgments

The authors wish to thank the following people, our highly experienced project team, for their deeply valuable contributions to the development of this manuscript:

- **Karen Pryor**, editor—for once again giving so much of her time, energy, and brilliant writing insights to all aspects of this manuscript. If this book makes sense and is useful to our readers, a great deal of that comes down to you and your wonderful way with words. Thank you, over and over.
- **Wayne Logue**, illustrator—for once again adding that critical extra layer of visual impact, which is so essential to communicating our message. We love sharing with the world your inspired, stimulating, and creative images, and we are deeply grateful to have had the honor of working with you. Thank you.
- **Cheryl Dick**, researcher—for once again helping us connect the dots, bringing together our ideas and the research that validates them. Without you, they would have been simply whimsical notions floating freely in the wind. With you, they have been grounded in what truly works in education. Thank you.

Publisher's Acknowledgments

Corwin wishes to acknowledge the following peer reviewers for their editorial insight and guidance.

Ellen E. Coulson
7th grade U.S. history teacher
Sig Rogich Middle School
Las Vegas, NV

Jane Hunn
8th grade general science teacher
Tippecanoe Valley Middle School
Akron, IN

Gayla LeMay
Middle school teacher
Louise Radloff Middle School
Duluth, GA

Tanya Marcinkewicz
6th grade science teacher
P. S. du Pont Middle School
Wilmington, DE

About the Authors

 **Rich Allen, PhD,** is a highly regarded educator with more than 25 years experience coaching teachers. Founder and president of Green Light Education, he is the author of numerous popular educational books, including most recently: *Sparking Student Synapses 9–12: Think Critically and Accelerate Learning* (2012); *High Five Teaching K–5: Using Green Light Strategies to Create Dynamic, Student-Focused Classrooms* (2011); *High-Impact Teaching Strategies for the 'XYZ' Era of Education* (2010); *Green Light Classrooms: Teaching Techniques That Accelerate Learning* (2008); and *TrainSmart: Effective Trainings Every Time* (2nd ed.) (2008). He has shared his dynamic instructional strategies not only in the United States and Canada, but also in such diverse countries as the United Kingdom, Australia, New Zealand, Hong Kong, Singapore, Thailand, Brunei, Russia, Jordan, and Brazil. Dr. Allen is also a popular keynote speaker at international education conferences and works with schools and school districts to embed effective teaching methods into mainstream curriculum.

Dr. Allen first took to the stage as an off-Broadway actor before starting his educational career as a high school math and drama teacher. In 1985, he became a lead facilitator for SuperCamp—an accelerated learning program for teens—and has since worked with more than 25,000 students worldwide. Dr. Allen completed his doctorate in educational psychology at Arizona State University, where he studied how the human brain receives, processes, and recalls information—knowledge that informs all aspects of his teaching strategies. The author divides his time between his home in the U.S. Virgin Islands on the sun-kissed paradise of St Croix, and his wife's home in Sydney, Australia, where he is learning to be a step-dad to two amazing young women. He can be reached at his email address: rich@drrichallen.com.

Jenn Currie has been teaching in the Commodore Perry School District for over 15 years, working largely with adolescents in Grades 4–6. Since discovering brain-based learning strategies in 2005, Jenn has consistently helped *problem* students achieve their first-ever academic successes. Her work has been recognized formally, as Teacher of the Year in 2008, 2011, and 2012, and informally through numerous letters from her students, their parents, and administrators.

After seeing powerful results in her own classroom, Jenn has become a staunch advocate of supporting student success through best practices and brain research. She has taken an increased role in professional development: facilitating workshops for parents, mentoring beginning teachers, leading professional study groups, as well as running in-service trainings at various school districts, universities, and state conferences. Since 2009, she has led a continuing education course entitled, "The Winning Combination: Linking Brain Research with Practical Classroom Strategies."

Jenn earned her BS and MEd in elementary education from Slippery Rock University of Pennsylvania and is currently pursuing a doctoral program in teaching and learning. Despite having taught for nearly two decades, she continues to delight in the challenge of showing every student that they *can* succeed.

Along with her husband, Scott, and their canine companion, Maggie, Jenn lives in the small, rural town of Greenville, Pennsylvania. Together they enjoy cooking and spending time in the great outdoors hiking, four-wheeling, and horseback riding. She may be reached at jenncurrie@verizon.net.

1

Why Many Middle School Students Need to Make a U-Turn

The expressions *middle school* and *middle years* are used fluidly within the educational arena, in some districts starting at Grade 4, in others going up to Grade 9. This book defines the middle years as Grades 5–8, taking a particular focus on the earlier, tricky 'tween years in middle school, when students are aged 9–12.

In education, these middle years mark a critical fork in the road when most students choose their direction in learning. Up until this point, a student's learning behaviors are fluid and can be molded fairly easily. But now these behaviors start to stiffen into unbending rigidity. In elementary school, we build the foundations of learning— the habits, work ethics, attitudes, self-beliefs, and assumptions that determine whether students will be enthusiastic, successful lifelong learners or reluctant underachievers. By the end of the middle years, these foundations may be firmly cemented into in place.

Thus, for us as teachers, the middle years are our last chance to put in place strong, positive learning patterns. If we don't break any negative and potentially destructive learning patterns and assumptions at this stage in a student's educational career, high school is likely to become one long and ultimately fruitless, battle—for teachers and students alike. Yet the opposite is equally true. If we embed positive, efficient, and effective patterns of learning in the middle years, students are far more likely to succeed in high school and beyond.

This book is called *U-Turn Teaching* because by the time they reach middle school, many students have started down a negative path on their educational journey. Most kids start off in a very positive direction in terms of their early attitudes toward school, learning, their fellow classmates, and teachers. They greet their initial school experiences eagerly, and—in the early days at least—few are disappointed. In their first years of school, students are given enjoyable challenges that they can overcome with relative ease, and they are enthusiastically praised for their successes. They play and work in equal measure, in classrooms full of color, life, friends, and stories. For the vast majority of students, their early educational experiences are positive, upbeat, encouraging, and—best of all—filled with hope.

However, this euphoria doesn't last long. By the time students reach the middle years, the process of learning is changing from curiosity, engagement, and hands on exploration to one of sitting still, listening, and writing. As this change happens, a student's enthusiasm for school and learning drops off rapidly. Exactly when this occurs will vary, depending on the student, the teachers, the curriculum, or even the dictates of the school district. But it almost always happens, eventually. And when it does, many students start to head down a negative path from which we, as teachers, must help them make a U-turn.

Traditionally, a U-turn is defined as *performing a 180-degree rotation to reverse the direction of travel.*

This is **exactly** what we need middle school students to do—because by high school, it's often too late to get them back on the road to success. The further students travel down the negative track, the harder it is for them to retrace their steps and recapture positive learning habits. If frustration, humiliation, and failure are the predominant themes in middle school students' lives, they will only become further alienated and less successful in high school. However, if we can steer students into a U-turn and help them regain their initial interest in and enthusiasm for learning during the middle years, these qualities have an excellent chance of continuing to flourish in high school.

Clearly, if we wish to produce successful students, the middle years are pivotal. While the forge is still ablaze, and the iron of student behavior is still malleable, we must strike—and strike hard—to reverse any unhelpful patterns of learning development. So, how do we do that? How do we reengage these students in the learning process, adjust their attitudes, and foster confidence and success?

We need a new approach that deals with the unique developmental phase these students are going through. They are no longer children, but not quite teenagers. They are maturing as people, but definitely not mature. They are not ready for the adult sink-or-swim teaching strategies of high school; yet, they no longer need the intensive support afforded to younger students. This age group needs strong guidance, but enough freedom to think for themselves. Students must learn to take responsibility, while also knowing they are completely supported by their teacher.

To teach this age group appropriately and help struggling students to make a U-turn, middle school teachers clearly require different teaching strategies. Such strategies are the focus of this book: How teachers can help middle school students get back on the path toward successful life-long learning, and how to anchor those behaviors firmly in place, so they will withstand the pressure-cooker environment of high school.

Making a U-Turn in Your Teaching

For many readers, these new strategies will require educators themselves to make a U-turn in their teaching—to do many things in their classroom that are 180 degrees different from their current practice. And teachers should welcome this chance because it offers them an opportunity to rekindle their own enthusiasm for and love of teaching.

Just as most students start off their educational careers with positive expectations, most teachers start off their teaching careers bursting with enthusiasm. They are eager for the opportunity to put the strategies they learned in their teacher-training program into practice. They are excited by the chance to make a difference, to affect the future, and to see that glow of excitement on a child's face when he suddenly finds success. They are willing to do whatever it takes to make this happen, so they study hard, learn the *right* ways to teach, and earn their certificate.

And, indeed, they start their first teaching position aiming to always teach in the most effective way possible, to do their best in every moment of every day, and to give every child an equal chance to succeed. However, often within the first few months of their first teaching experience, something unexpected happens. These lofty goals disappear into the swirling vortex of school life. And into this same vortex go all thoughts and considerations about adjusting teaching practices to meet an individual student's needs. Instead, what takes over is a simple need to survive. To do so, new teachers quickly adopt different habits, using practices seen in other classrooms around the school—practices that, from the outside at least, appear to result in *good teaching*.

For example, consider the common idea that middle school students learn best working quietly at their desks. While movement is often accepted as a normal part of the elementary school classroom, by the time students reach the middle years it is often thought they should be perfectly ready to sit and work quietly—and if they aren't ready, then now is the time they should learn how.

From the outside perspective, it's easy to understand why making students work sitting at their desks in silence seems utterly reasonable. Any visitor to this classroom would see a perfect picture of what they remember as ideal learning conditions: students sitting quietly. Clearly, these students are learning something; obviously, these students have a good teacher!

Yet, we now know that for the majority of students, sitting quietly for long stretches of time actively prohibits understanding and recall. Over thirty years of careful research (Hattie, 2009, p. 212) into how the human brain learns has revealed the importance of students moving and talking in the classroom. The teaching practice of making students "work quietly at their desks," while producing an admirable scene for the casual visitor, does little to support learning, and is likely to produce some very damaging outcomes—for students and teacher alike. Here are five of the many, less-than-positive, results:

1. The practice excludes the 35–40% of kinesthetic learners in the classroom who do not learn unless they are moving. These will be the first students to become restless and disruptive, starting a ripple of distraction in the room as the teacher fights to keep these students under control. Most of these disruptive students will not learn the material, and many of the remaining students will become distracted.

2. Preventing students from talking reduces the likelihood of them embedding the new material in their long-term memory. Transferring information from our short to our long-term memory requires *processing*. For some students, figuring out the worksheet will be sufficient processing to encode the memory. But for many students, this level of processing only occurs when they talk. Working in silence deprives them of this critical processing step, resulting in them quickly losing all memory of the new material.

3. For the students excluded in the previous two outcomes, the experience plants the seed of, or reinforces, a destructive false assumption: *I cannot succeed at learning*. Many of these students are perfectly capable of academic success—if they are taught in an appropriate way that allows them to move or talk. However, if their teacher continues to rely on lecture and silent worksheet activities as the primary mode of information delivery and learning practice, these students will finish middle school firmly established as underachievers in both their and their teachers' minds.

4. Because over half the class has failed to adequately learn the material, the teacher must now set aside additional classroom time to reteach the same material.

5. The need to discipline students, as well as the need to reteach content that students should already know, is incredibly frustrating for the teacher.

It's easy to see how these damaging outcomes gradually create a viscous downward spiral. The more the classroom becomes a battleground, the more irritated and exhausted the teacher becomes. And there is no way to win. Firmer discipline may result in a quieter class-room—but it will NOT create better results. Teaching stops being a joy and becomes a struggle. Good teachers start to question their calling.

This is when you know it's time to make a U-turn in your teaching practices—for your own sake, as well as for your students—a U-turn that harnesses the science of brain-based learning.

Brain-Based Learning

The phrase *brain-based learning* has been overused—as well as misused—with alarming frequency in the last thirty years. When research on how the brain learns was in its infancy, the term was fairly well restricted to a few key issues that were being carefully studied. Researchers were rightfully cautious about making broad generalizations regarding their discoveries. However, especially in the past decade, the term *brain-based learning* has expanded to encompass an incredibly wide range of educational ideas that are essentially just good, sound, fundamental teaching practices. Understandably, many teachers feel that brain-based learning is a fad that has had its day. Yet, the original science and the wealth of new research expanding the field are extremely sound. We know how the human brain processes and remembers information—and no one is disputing the validity of these discoveries—so we should use these facts to increase success in our classrooms.

This book takes the term back to its original intent:

> *Brain-based learning means what researchers have discovered about how the brain learns best, and how that directly relates to effective classroom learning.*

All the ideas and strategies in this book are based on what we now know about how the brain processes and remembers information.

Yet, while we cite this research at various points through this book, it is not a comprehensive overview of research about the human brain. Instead, we have a singular focus: *to translate what has been discovered in the area of brain research into practical, doable classroom strategies.* While the research provides a wonderful starting point for understanding how educators can most effectively reach students, it is only that—a starting point. We still have to translate these wonderful insights into how people learn into workable, daily teaching practices.

Guiding Insights

Here are the *guiding insights* from brain-based research that form the threads of the tapestry that underlies all of the strategies and techniques offered throughout this book—the first two will be familiar! These insights are stated in a less technical way than some researchers might prefer, but since this is a book about practical application, let us start by stating them the language of the classroom.

Insight	Why It's Important	What It Means to You
Movement is vital (Van Praag, Kempermann, & Gage, 1999, pp. 266–270)	Movement increases blood flow, which increases oxygen levels in the brain—leading to better focus, attention, and engagement.	At all times, find reasons for your students to move.
Student conversations enhance learning	Talking is one of the most powerful means of processing new information.	Let students process information with their peers whenever possible.
Experiential learning works (Sousa & Tomlinson, 2011, p. 14)	Total engagement—mental, physical, and emotional—directly leads to higher levels of learning and recall.	Whenever possible, include an experiential component in your lessons.
Memory strategies are important	Most students need a specific recall method to retrieve a memory.	When introducing new information, build in a moment when you explicitly tell your students: *Here's how we will remember this.*
Redundant retrieval routes boost recall	When students have *more than one* way to remember key information, they find it easier to remember.	Try to create audio, visual, kinesthetic, and emotional memories of new content.
Positive emotions support learning (Sousa & Tomlinson, 2011, p. 20)	Students learn best when they are happy. Fear, anger, and stress literally shut down our ability to learn.	Proactively seek to create anticipation, curiosity, excitement, joy, and laughter.

To any experienced teacher, few of these guiding insights will be stunning revelations. When you think back on your most successful lessons, you will probably see quite a few of these strategies woven through those experiences—whether you included them consciously or not.

The bottom line is that these ideas are important—they matter—and we need to be conscious of them to ensure we are on the right path. To design effective, dynamic lessons, and understand how to run the middle school classroom efficiently and competently, we must keep coming back to these guiding insights.

Clearly, this is not an exhaustive list. We have cherry-picked from a wealth of findings to give you what we believe are the most salient research-based insights into learning. For our purposes, we wanted the list to be precise, concise, and manageable. The ones we included are the largest, most broadly important factors in the strategies shown throughout this book.

Some readers may point out, correctly, that research also shows that the absolute fastest way to teach someone something is through pain-aversion (Johansen, Fields, & Manning, 2001). This is why most people only need to touch a hot stove once to learn not to touch it again! And why military training—where a person's ability to stay alive can depend on how fast they learn—is often extremely brutal.

However, given the overarching goal of our education system is to create lifelong learners, this approach is not appropriate in the classroom. Pain-aversion learning brings with it a host of negative, wide-ranging reactions and responses that would quickly spread to all areas of classroom learning—something we dearly want to avoid.

This is why the starting point for U-Turn teaching is to create a positive learning environment. A well thought out and carefully run classroom, full of laughter, noise, and fun, creates a host of connected *positive* reactions and responses that we can leverage to help our students succeed.

To achieve this, you don't have to make every guiding insight a part of every moment of every lesson. Such a lesson would be impractical to design, and impossible to conduct in the classroom. These guiding insights are not *must haves*, but frequently recurring and intertwining themes—rarely does one operate solely on its own.

If you are interested in finding out about more of the research behind each of these guiding insights, we have provided a few citations to get you started. You'll soon discover an enormous amount of brain-based research behind each of these ideas. Right now, it's time to start discovering how we can put these insights, from all the wonderful brain-based research, to use in our classrooms.

Teaching With Intention

First and foremost: Stay aware of the guiding insights. Deliberately take these facts about how the human brain processes information and see what they mean to your teaching practices. Examine what's happening in your classroom through the lens of the insights. You might start to see apparently bad behavior in a different light (Boynton & Boynton, 2005, p. 5). Students rarely act out because they are *bad*—they act out because they are uncomfortable and disengaged. Stop saying *no* and starting asking *why?*

Next, look at the following four principles which are the primary focus of this book. They are designed to focus you on how to intentionally put brain research (Hattie, 2009, p. 119) to use in your middle school classroom:

1. **Build and maintain trust**—If they are to achieve academic success, students must first feel safe in their environment.

2. **Create a collaborative community**—Harness the power of collaboration to improve learning outcomes; encourage acceptance and tolerance, and instill personal responsibility.

3. **Take a TEAMing approach**—Working together improves emotional safety and enables students to better process information (Frey, Fisher, & Everlove, 2009, p. 58).

4. **Prime the positive environment**—The easiest way to maintain discipline is to reinforce and reward good behavior.

This book devotes the next four chapters to each of these principles, covering the theory behind them and providing a range of practical strategies for embedding them into the fabric of your classroom.

Please know that these strategies have been tested in both self-contained and departmentalized classrooms—and in all middle school grade levels. For simplicity, they are often described in a self-contained context, with notes on how to adapt for departmentalized teaching. They are also typically described for use in the early middle school classrooms (Grades 5 and 6), because this is where students need the most coaching and modeling. You can easily adapt them for more mature students by omitting any steps that seem too elementary. The key is to understand the intent behind the strategy, and then to implement it in a way that will work with *your* students in *your* classroom.

Much like the guiding insights, the four principles depend on each other, and overlap in various places. Therefore, here is a very brief introduction to each one, so you'll be aware of the interplay between them, regardless of which chapter you read first.

Build and Maintain Trust

Trust is among the most important values in any relationship, and the teacher-student relationship is no exception. Yet in a classroom, the issue is magnified since student-to-student relationships must also be maintained on a trusting level. Indeed, the fact that so many student-to-student and teacher-student relationships must be simultaneously managed to develop a trusting environment makes this an enormously powerful—and vitally critical—part of any successful middle school classroom. Of even more importance, the middle years are the development stage in which students first truly experience their sense of self-worth and its relationship to their peers. Sustaining trust under these circumstances requires clearly established rituals and routines to build trust at all levels. This chapter not only outlines these important rituals and routines, but also shows how they are used in practical situations. You'll find ways to vary the rituals so they remain fresh and interesting, a number of new and imaginative places where trust can be further developed, far beyond what's normally expected in a traditional classroom.

Create a Collaborative Community

When students work in collaboration with each other, it often leads rapidly to a higher level of understanding and insight than would be possible if the teacher were merely explaining new concepts. Often, a student struggling to make sense of an idea may understand it better when it is explained by a peer (who only recently figured it out herself) rather than by an adult. Collaborative learning succeeds at multiple levels, with students often feeling they are not having to learn in the traditional sense. In addition, students who work in cooperative groups learn to respect and value each other's different strengths, styles, and needs. This chapter looks at how to physically change the set-up of the room to enhance collaborative moments, as well as explaining a variety of collaborative learning activities. Using these classroom set-ups and activities results in middle school students learning to work together, respect each other, and build a dynamic community of learners.

Take a TEAMing Approach

Evidence suggests that teams create a supportive network, lowering blood pressure, improving immune systems, and driving attention. Teams provide a predictable transition between the students' world and the academic world, keeping stress levels low and eliminating threat responses. In addition, teams create a feeling of confidence, a sense of accomplishment and success, driving students to learn more, without extra effort by the teacher. And of course, teams can create the feeling of belonging, releasing positive brain chemicals such as serotonin, which make students calmer and happier (Wolk, 2008, p. 10). Yet while the success of the teaming approach is rapidly gaining credibility in educational arenas, we need to know how to realistically make it work in a practical way in the classroom. This chapter offers a variety of concrete ways in which to establish, organize, and manage teams of middle school students. It brings to life the theoretical concept of teaming in the classroom, in a down-to-earth, realistic, highly practical way.

Prime the Positive Environment

This book advocates many teaching strategies that appear to threaten classroom discipline. For example, it positively encourages you to let your students move around, talk, laugh, and have fun. This chapter shows you how to allow all of these potentially chaotic activities, while still maintaining discipline, using a powerful self-reward system to reinforce good behavior. It is based on the proven premise that, by proactively demonstrating, facilitating, and motivating positive behavior, you can dramatically reduce the number of times you have to discipline your students. You'll also find strategies for handling occasional inappropriate behavior in a way that (1) does not embarrass the particular student, (2) does not unconsciously encourage the behavior in other students, (3) creates a positive outcome for the entire class, and (4) reduces the chances that those behaviors will occur in the future.

Once these four principles have been clearly explained and demonstrated through practical activities, the next section addresses how to bring together the various and sundry pieces into a complete package—a lesson that rocks. Lessons that truly work for middle school students, and classrooms that truly work for the students and the teacher, are the eventual aim of everything offered in the book.

The U-Turn Is Vital

For many middle school students, the frightening truth is that it's not just time for a U-turn in their attitudes toward learning—it's their last chance. By the time they reach high school, their lives will be filled with content-specific schoolwork to complete, athletic opportunities to seize, social demands to be met, and much, much more. If they are not on the right path, with the proper attitude toward learning, when they depart middle school, it may well be too late. For there's a strong chance that no one will ever focus as closely on them as an individual again, and they will be lost forever in the greater shuffle of high school life.

As a middle school teacher, you have a chance to, literally, change lives. By using the ideas and strategies in this book, you can help middle school students to make a U-turn on their educational paths, opening up a world of possibilities. And, in the process, you may also find yourself making a U-turn back to your original love of teaching. Because knowing how to open those doors of possibilities for your students—putting them on a positive path to better and more successful lives—is really the most that any teacher, at any level, could ever ask for.

Let the U-Turn begin right now.

2

Creating and Maintaining Trust

Trust is the glue that binds relationships together (Cleveland, 2011, p. 69). It underlies all of our positive and successful relationships, from professional to personal, from casual to intimate. Across the board, the relationships we value most are built on a rock-solid foundation of trust in the other person—trust that they will care about our needs and make decisions in our best interest. When we trust people, we value their opinions and listen to their advice; these are the people with whom we celebrate success and who we turn to when things go wrong.

Trust is also vital for a successful student-teacher relationship. Learning may appear to be an intellectual exercise; but in terms of the educational experience, learning is—at its heart—*emotional*. This is because learning is a voyage of discovery, requiring us to venture into the unknown. Along the way, it requires us to try things for the first time—an inherently risky undertaking. This means that, in every step of the learning journey, we face the very real risk we will not succeed. Indeed, most of us will fail several times before we master a concept. For many people, the process of trying and failing, and trying again is a primary method of learning. We literally do learn from our mistakes. In fact, we cannot learn if we are not willing to fail.

As teachers, we must recognize the emotional leap of faith it takes for our students to fully engage with learning—to deliberately risk failure. If we expect them to run this potentially humiliating risk, we must provide them with an emotional safety net (Zapf, 2008, p. 68). Meaning, they must trust us to support them, to believe in them, and to provide them with a safe classroom culture where failure is not ridiculed or punished, but simply seen as a healthy part of the learning process.

Just as we wouldn't attempt to cross a tight rope without first putting up a safety net, so we cannot expect our students to tackle a new concept without first establishing trust. Trust is the most important educational enabler; it is the starting point from which flows all the positive emotions—curiosity, surprise, laughter—so vital to creating and maintaining a successful learning environment.

Unfortunately, by the time students reach middle school, trust is harder to achieve in the classroom because of the massive power imbalance in the teacher's favor. After all, the teacher is the assigned authority figure in the learning process, holding the knowledge the student must learn. The teacher chooses when and how the student learns the new information, sets tasks, and assesses success. The teacher can offer reward or punishment, incentive or deterrent, praise or criticism. In any sphere of learning, the teacher holds the power.

For younger students, this is not a problem. Very young children have a wonderful faith in their teacher's inherent goodness and wisdom. However, by middle school, many kids have started questioning a teacher's authority. This is a perfectly natural part in the process of attaining a *sense of self*. To oversimplify an important developmental phase, this means middle school students are striving to find their niche, their place in the world where they feel significant. They need to feel they belong and have something to contribute. If they can't make their mark in some positive way, they will distinguish themselves by acting out. This does not mean they're bad kids; they've just never been shown a positive way to make their mark in the world.

The issue middle school teachers must grapple with is that in the late preschool years and early school years, sense of self is usually associated with attributes modeled by parents and teachers. However, by middle school, peer values and peer pressure play an increasingly influential role in how students think about themselves. Thus, these students are more likely to question a teacher's authority. Rather than thinking, "The teacher is right," they are more likely to think, "The teacher is boring," "The teacher is unfair," "The teacher doesn't like me," "The teacher thinks I'm dumb."

The upshot is most middle school students find it hard to trust someone who appears to have absolute control over their destiny. At this age, the imbalance of power in the classroom stresses the already fragile bonds that keep trust intact and flowing freely.

As a result, middle school teachers have to put in an extraordinarily high level of extra effort to create and maintain trust within the learning process. This starts by being conscious of the potential for teachers to unwittingly abuse their position of power. Most teachers are usually startled (and horrified) at this suggestion. But consider the following, extremely common situation: A student is becoming increasingly restless while seated at his desk, disturbing other students. In a stern voice, their teacher orders him to sit still and work quietly. If this is not the first incident, or if the student keeps on fidgeting, the teacher might even direct the student to go and sit out in the hallway until he settles down.

The problem with this approach is that the teacher has effectively dealt with the situation by using her position of power. Because a teacher *can* say "Don't do that!" he or she hasn't bothered to find out *why* the student is behaving that way. Perhaps the student needs to go to the bathroom. Perhaps, like half the rest of the class, a student finds sitting still in a hard chair for longer than fifteen minutes really uncomfortable. Perhaps they need to get up and stretch. Perhaps they are simply acting out. Regardless, the teacher doesn't bother to find out. And the response sends a subliminal—and very damaging—message: "I'm not interested in why you're behaving that way. I don't care about your needs." The implied lack of desire to seek out a solution breaks trust with the student on an unconscious, yet vitally important, level. The student wonders: "If they don't care enough to help me here, do they really care about me at all?"

To build trust, we must consciously take every opportunity to send the opposite message. In this type of situation, instead of barking, "Don't do that!" we must take the time to engage with the student and find a solution. Perhaps, in this case, the teacher might invite the student, and anyone else who wishes, to stand up and work at their desks, or take thirty seconds to stand up a stretch. While this may require time and energy, the rewards can be huge. When students recognize that teachers are going out of their way to meet their needs, trust grows—a confidence that this person, this *adult*, really recognizes and understands their needs. This trust then spills over into other areas in the learning process, creating a chain reaction of numerous positive results.

> *"I've come to the frightening conclusion that I am the decisive element in the classroom. It's my daily mood that makes the weather. As a teacher, I possess a tremendous power to make a child's life miserable or joyous. I can be a tool of torture or an instrument of inspiration. I can humiliate or humor, hurt or heal. In all situations, it is my response that decides whether a crisis will be escalated or de-escalated and a child humanized or de-humanized."*
>
> —Haim Ginott

This is just one, tiny example to illustrate the bigger, on-going, ever-present issue of maintaining teacher-student trust. Every choice we make as teachers, at every level, sends a message to our students, continuously affecting trust levels in our classrooms. Every time we respond or act, we are either building or destroying trust. So we need to stop and think: What message am I sending? This need to be aware of our microactions may seem overwhelming, but remember: No one gets it right, all the time, every time. Just be aware, the more our students see us demonstrating that their needs are important, the more they will trust us.

When middle-year students truly trust their teachers, they bring an astonishing level of focus to their efforts, creating the opportunity to learn easily and rapidly. This is why the following chapter is devoted entirely to *trust*. It offers practical, proactive ideas for building trust, not only between the teacher and the student, but between students as well—the kind of trust that truly allows students to engage and achieve at their highest levels.

How to Establish Trust

Trust develops when students feel that they are a valued part of a family or team (Tomlinson, 2008, p. 28). Three aspects of our classroom environment help to create this feeling: safety, ownership, and rituals.

Safety

We must convince our students that their efforts to learn will be supported and not met with ridicule from us or their peers. This requires considerable effort at the beginning of the year to set up safety nets to support students in taking the risks required to learn new skills. Here are ten ideas to help you put and keep these safety nets in place.

1. Before-school letter

2. Survival kits

3. Traveling supplies

4. No Tone Zone

5. Teach them how they learn

6. "I will not let you fail"

7. —Save Our Student

8. Get real

9. Success from the start

10. Make it predictable

Before-School Letter

Many teachers already send out before-school letters, offering a useful place to start building trust even before school begins. Basically, about a month before the first day of school, send out a letter or postcard welcoming the students to your class. As shown in the example, your letter can detail any supplies students can usefully bring in. However, its more important purpose is to tell students that you have heard good things about them and are looking forward to teaching them.

Dear _____,

We sixth grade teachers hope this letter finds you having a great summer! We've noticed all the school supplies are back in the stores . . . have you? Are you scoping them out yet? We certainly have!

Together we have pulled together a list of supplies that would be *nice to have* to make the school year run smoothly. This way, if you and your family *want* to purchase back-to-school items, you won't be buying unnecessary things.

Of course, the school provides all the "big stuff" like pencils, paper, glue, rulers, assignment books, a 3-ring binder, and homework folders. All the items listed below are available at Big Lots, Dollar Tree, or Wal-Mart. We tried finding the best prices in town. If possible, please bring them with you on the first day of school.

- (1) 1-subject notebook ($.20)
- (1 pad) sticky notes ($1)
- (1 pkg.) 3 × 5 lined index cards ($.64)
- (1) pencil box (smallish, easy to carry and manage: $.57)
- (1 pkg. of 3) Pocket Pads (mini pocket tablets) ($1)
- (1 pkg.) highlighters/4 colors ($1.47)
- (2) Marble Composition Books (black and white book with sewn binding) ($.40 each)
- (4) LARGE cloth book covers for all texts ($.57–$1.97 each)
- (optional) 12-pack of colored pencils ($.74)
- (optional) tissues
- (optional) anti-bacterial wipes
- (optional but FUN!) old sports/suit coat—we will become "Reading and Writing Detectives" this year, so we must dress the part! Raid your dad's, step-dad's, or grandpa's closet for an old, never-going-to-be-worn-again jacket!

We are looking forward to a GREAT school year! We hear wonderful things about **you**. Be prepared to experience things you have never experienced before in school like learning about the brain and cool Science labs! J If you have any questions, please e-mail your homeroom teacher at [teacher e-mail address] or [teacher e-mail address]. We look forward to seeing you bright and early on _____.

Until then,

_____

Survival Kits

On the first day of school, create a warm welcome by putting an individually named "Survival Kit" on each desk. These can be Chinese containers or small paper bags containing a few inexpensive goodies. Critically, each item in the kit must represent a "Key to Success" in your classroom. See table below for ideas, including some very low cost items to make this affordable in departmentalized classrooms. Note—you don't have to use all of these items, just a few that work for you with your students.

The named kit serves three initial (if secondary) purposes: it tells students where to sit, piques their curiosity, and creates a common interest. They are dying to know what's in the container. Also, the message is clear: *This is going to be an interesting year!*

Item	*Message*	*Discussion*
Oops erasers, available by the gross from ForTeachersOnly.com	Mistakes are good!	*It's OK to make mistakes; in fact we all learn better and become smarter by correcting those mistakes. In this classroom, we are never embarrassed by making mistakes.*
Mini slinky, bendable character, or pipe cleaner	Be flexible!	*When we work with partners, you may find yourself working with someone you may not care for or whose ideas you disagree with. This is a part of life—you have to be prepared to compromise. Remember: these partnerships are only temporary. I'm not asking you to marry the person, just work with them for a few minutes.*
Mint, gem (you can find bags of them in craft stores), or clappers (from party stores)	Be encouraging!	*Everyone needs a little encouragement to make it through the day. Tell your teammates they're doing a good job or that they'll get it eventually.*
		Brainstorm ideas of what students might say, e.g. Nice try, you'll get it next time!
Brain eraser pencil topper	Two heads are better than one!	*Some days, we may not 'have our heads on straight.' Thank goodness we have teammates who can lend us a hand with their 'brainy' ideas! In this class, we will work together, share ideas, collaborate, and build off one another. We all bring a different perspective to the table. With the combination of all our ideas, we will learn more!*

Item	Message	Discussion
Piece of string	Pull together!	*The string is like a student. It's hard to push string along, but we can easily PULL on it. In this class, we pull each other along with positive words, rather than pushing with criticism. [Note: You could introduce this item using the video Pulling Together from simpletruths.com.]*
$100 magnetic book mark	Give 100%!	*To truly get the most out of school, we need to put our full effort into everything we do! Give 100% and you will achieve more than you believe possible.*
Smiley guys	Always up!	*In this class, we always find something to smile about.*
Fuzzy puff ball (from craft stores)	No Tone Zone!	*Keep your comments soft. We don't use a 'tone' with our fellow classmates.*
Dice	Take chances!	*The best learning comes when you are brave enough to risk getting something wrong. In this classroom, when you take a chance, we will applaud your courage!*
Life Saver candy	Save Our Student!	*When you are stuck, you can always count on someone to help you.*
Mascot—e.g., picture or plastic toy	We're a team!	*In this classroom, we're a team. And every team needs a mascot. This is our mascot. You'll see him around the classroom in different places. He's there to remind you that you belong!*

The primary purpose of the kit is to use the items as the jumping off point for a series of short discussions that will make students feel safe in your classroom. You can either explain the significance of each item all at once or discuss a couple every day. It's helpful for younger students to keep a *kit key*, where they record each meaning, or you can put a poster on the wall as a reminder.

Once you have discussed all the items and their meanings with your students, use the following activity to cement the understanding of each concept: Give pairs an index card with a *key term* written on it. The pairs have ten to fifteen minutes to create a skit that demonstrates their Key to Success. The remaining members of the class guess which key they are playing.

Once established, refer back to these keys to success whenever appropriate, using positive examples you see and hear around the class. It's important to make these principles real for your students. If they see them in action all the time, they will believe in them too.

Traveling Supplies

You probably already have a drawer of extra school supplies available for any student who needs them. To support your students who don't have resources at home, why not extend this to include a stash of traveling supplies? These are pencil boxes filled with colored pencils, markers, glue stick, and scissors that any student can take home overnight. This simple intervention demonstrates to students that your support extends beyond the classroom.

No Tone Zone

From the start, make it clear that your classroom is a No Tone Zone. This simply means just that, when speaking to each other, a sarcastic or condescending tone will not be tolerated.

Introduce this idea in the first week of school through a class discussion. First, as a group, talk about how the tone of our voice, or the particular comments we say could hurt a person's feeling, whether we meant to or not. Discuss how, just because we may be having a bad day, this doesn't give us the permission to snap or snarl at our classmates. Next, introduce the idea that everyone has strengths and weaknesses, and our job as a class is to help everyone improve. So when we witness a weakness in another, we lend a hand and help strengthen those weaknesses—we don't make sarcastic remarks.

End the discussion by modeling how to communicate respectfully and how to respond when someone uses a hurtful tone. You might give as an example:

Cameron, the tone of your voice is condescending and hurtful. It makes a person feel dumb. Please rephrase what you just said to Jason in a more pleasant voice.

Classroom Snapshot

A few weeks into the No Tone Zone . . .

Journey (in a sarcastic voice):	*Yeah, Dan, you were supposed to clean that up!*
Dan:	*Journey, that remark you just made is what Mrs. Currie considers a TONE!*
Journey (with a sheepish look):	*Sorry Dan, you are right. I'll help you clean up.*

Teach Them How They Learn

On the very first day of school, explain to your students how they learn—about the different needs of kinesthetic, audio, and visual learners and the existence of memory strategies. Make it clear that if students don't understand or remember, this isn't because they're *dumb*, it's because they haven't found the right learning mode or memory strategy yet.

For most students, this is a revelation. It's a vital step in creating trust because it shares the responsibility for learning between student and teacher. Plus, it enhances learning; once students understand there are many ways to understand new information—and actual strategies for remembering it—they are less likely to give up if they fail the first time.

"I Will Not Let You Fail."

You can build on this idea of shared responsibility for learning—and cement the trust between you and your students—by promising them: *I will not let you fail.* Sometimes, you need to literally say this to a student who is upset that they can't grasp a concept. Other times, you can demonstrate this principle by showing students that making mistakes is a vitally important part of learning. As often as possible, reinforce the Key to Success message that mistakes are good.

One of the biggest fears for kids at school is that they will be left behind—they will be the person who comes last or the only one who misses a particular problem. If you're checking answers orally, when someone gives an incorrect answer, first make it clear that's OK and that others found the question hard too. You can even say, "I bet there is at least one other person who missed it too." Often someone will pipe up and share that they too got the answer wrong or found the question tricky.

Tell your students that to learn from an error, they must instantly correct it on their paper; that way, they will remember not to make that mistake again. If they continue to make mistakes without being made to feel foolish, eventually students will relax and stop being fearful of getting the answer wrong. With that fear erased, your students will be prepared, even eager, to take risks in their learning. They won't be afraid to question or disagree with others—because they know it's OK to make a mistake.

Classroom Snapshot

One day, Danielle breaks down in math, tears streaming down her cheeks. She tells me she's terrible at math—she will never get this. I sit down beside her and we talk. After listening for a while, I tell her I have great faith in her, and I promise her: *No matter what, I will not let you fail. It's my job to make sure you get this concept!*

I also tell her that her brain can't do math while she's upset. So, the first step to success is for her to relax and trust me that she will get this. It may not be today, but we'll continue to hit on it and it will come . . . I guarantee it! Second, she needs a change of scene. I tell her to go take a walk to the restroom, wipe her face, get a drink, and take a few deep breaths. Come back when she is calm and ready, and she and I will start again.

The second time, she finds it a bit easier. It's not perfect, but she is on her way to conquering the concept. By the following week, she has mastered it completely.

Years later, Danielle still talks about that day and thanks me for letting her know I wouldn't leave her behind.

S.O.S.—Save Our Student

To further remove the fear of making mistakes, introduce the S.O.S. system. If students are unable to answer a question or problem on their own, or correct their mistakes while working orally, they can simply call for assistance, or S.O.S., from another classmate. This stops students from having to make an embarrassing guess or admitting they don't know. It offers a safety net that encourages even the most timid students to have a go at working something out on the board—because they know, if they get stuck, a classmate will come to their rescue.

SAVE OUR STUDENT

Classroom Snapshot

Jason Casteel (age 11) to another student who is obviously struggling with a problem: *It's OK to make a mistake in here Kacee. We'll always come to your rescue. Just call S.O.S.*

Get Real

The exciting thing about building trust with middle schoolers is that it's a huge opportunity to teach students, especially the younger ones, to recognize and respect the feelings of others. These students need to learn how to consider the needs and feelings of others and make appropriate responses when people need support—starting with their teacher. This requires teachers to *get real* with their students and share with them some (appropriate) realities of life. For example, middle school students are usually stunned to discover their teacher is a regular human being, someone who gets nervous when the principal walks in, is tired from grading papers or sad when they have to put their cat to sleep.

Here are a few opportunities to start you thinking about what you might share with your students.

- *Tell them about your school days*—Struggling students assume learning is easy for everyone else but them. You can remove this unhelpful assumption by telling them about the subjects you found hard at school. Telling anecdotes about your own educational trials creates an important bond of shared experience. It's never occurred to your students that you might understand what they're going through. Your candor will encourage them to tell you as soon as they start struggling—a much better moment to fill learning gaps than after the test.
- *Be honest about bad days*—Where appropriate, tell your students if you're having a bad day. Perhaps you're not feeling well, or you've had bad news. If you ask your students to be kind and patient, and tell them why; the mood will shift and your students will respond. They will be quieter, reflective, and concerned, making it easier for you to get through the day and teaching them an important lesson in thinking about others.
- *Point out to students when their behavior is affecting others*—If a student is acting out of character and being rude, rather than taking them on in public, have a quiet chat behind the scenes. You can say, "I'm not exactly sure what is going on with you today, but my

feelings are really hurt by the way you are talking to me." Generally, your student will not have realized his or her actions were affecting how you felt. If you have your students' trust, they will quickly apologize and change their behavior.

Success From the Start

Here's a great way to lay the foundations for trust. On the first day of school, give your students proof positive that they can learn by teaching them the memory peg system (visit www.richallen.co.nz and click on "Memory Pegs" for instructions on how to do this in a fast, fun way). Within fifteen minutes, every student can learn the system and use it to memorize a list of twenty items—a feat most of them thought completely impossible. This almost magical experience of mind blowing success teaches students a vitally important lesson—in your classroom, they can succeed!

By middle school, most students have pigeonholed themselves as a particular type of learner. Some of the students in your class will already truly believe they are dumb. Many others will believe they are OK at this, but bad at that. It's important to shatter any limiting negative assumptions as quickly as possible and build self-belief. You want all students in your classroom to believe they can succeed, no matter what their previous educational experience. This simple, fun, and attainable accomplishment opens students' eyes to an ability they may have never considered possible, as well as proving that *everyone* is capable of learning.

Classroom Snapshot

You're right Mrs. Currie! I really do remember 90% of these words better now that I tie them to pictures! I'm going to do this all the time now! —Alan Jablonski (age 11)

Make It Predictable

Having a predictable classroom lowers your students' stress levels, supporting their learning. To help make your classroom feel safe, try to maintain a predictable schedule your students can count on. If you know there will be a break in your normal schedule, try to tell your students the day before or post it on your message board (see page 36). In particular, if you know you're going to be absent, give your students as much warning as possible and clarify what they will be doing while you're away.

Ownership

The second stage of building trust is to make students feel at home by sending clear messages that it's their classroom (Guskey & Anderman, 2008, p. 8). This is best achieved in the first week through a series of specific activities designed to increase students' feeling of ownership:

- Team towers
- They build the rules (Guskey & Anderman, 2008, p. 12).
- We are all a piece of the puzzle
- Classroom scavenger hunt
- Morning greeting
- Get to know you

Team Towers

Use a team building activity that leads to a discussion about what it takes to work together successfully, which in turn will help your students comes up with their own classroom rules. For example, teams of three or four are given ten minutes to build the tallest, free-standing tower they can out of twenty-five drinking straws and two inches of masking tape. Generally, at least one team fails to construct a successful tower, offering clues as to what *not* to do.

To debrief the activity, ask the successful teams: "What did your team do that allowed you to construct such a magnificent tower?" Typically, this elicits comments such as, "Well, we talked out the process first . . . We listened to everybody's ideas first, and then decided which seemed most feasible . . . We tried one person's idea, it didn't work, so we switched to another person's idea . . . and it worked!"

Then go back to the less successful teams: "It appears things didn't go so well over here. What do you attribute the problem to?" Often, students say, "We couldn't decide on whose ideas to choose . . . We argued . . . We all wanted to be the boss."

This creates the perfect segue into part two of this activity— drawing up rules for teamwork.

They Build the Rules

Typically, teachers have a barrage of rules and expectations outlined and posted on their classroom wall on the first day of school. Instead, to move from *my* room to *our* room, hand the responsibility for rule building over to your students. This simple yet empowering act translates into: *I trust and value your voice, and I believe in your decision making ability.* It also has the side benefit of making students more willing to abide by the rules, because they made them.

After your team tower building contest and its ensuing discussion, ask each team to generate a list of qualities that make successful teams. Overnight, combine the suggestions into one giant list.

The next day, give a copy of the giant list to each team and ask them to cut it apart and organize the ideas into similar piles. Generally four or five underlying themes fall out of this activity. Based on these piles, ask the teams to come up with rules that mirror their piles.

Post each team's four or five rules on the board—generally the main rules are very similar, just stated differently. As a class, decide how to best state these key classroom principles to make your final list. If you have a classroom theme or mascot, you could try to use it as an acronym. For example, if your mascot is a gecko, your rules might end up like this:

G = Get along

E = Everyone is included

C = Curiosity

K = Kind to each other

O = Outstanding work!

Once you reach a consensus, put your final list of rules up on the wall and ask all students to sign the paper to show they agree and vow to respect those rules. Finally, with all signatures present, make copies for everyone to keep in their binders as a gentle reminder.

The great thing about student-generated rules is that, at any given moment, you can pull them out and say, "Hey, you all agreed to be kind to each other. Today, I am not seeing it. How are we going to make this better?" This simple yet effective method will become a cornerstone to creating a strong, cohesive community in your classroom.

We Are All Pieces of the Puzzle

For younger students, as a further community-building exercise, divide a large poster board into as many puzzle shaped pieces as there are people in the room (your students plus you) and cut them out. On the first day of school, give everyone a piece of the puzzle to decorate. A few days later, join together in the middle of the classroom with your puzzle pieces. Together, piece the puzzle together—not always an easy task. Often, the kinesthetic learners—frequently not book smart—are the ones with the best puzzling skills. This is a good moment for the rest of the class to value the peers who they might previously have looked down on. Once you have the entire puzzle together, tape it to the wall in the hallway with a sign that reads: WE ARE ALL A PIECE OF THE PUZZLE.

Debrief the activity by discussing how it took everyone's effort, pieces, and ideas to complete the puzzle. Talk about how, in this class, everyone is equally important and how everyone will succeed—together!

Classroom Scavenger Hunt

You need your students to quickly learn where everything is in the classroom, but rather than simply telling them, create a scavenger hunt where they must search the room for particular items they will use every day. This activity has the advantage of getting students up, moving, and engaged with their environment. Plus, if they have to locate materials, students are more likely to remember where they are than if you simply tell them.

Example of a Classroom Scavenger Hunt

- ✓ Where are the bathroom/hall passes located?
- ✓ Where do you find "extra" worksheet pages?
- ✓ Where can you find the word recess?
- ✓ How many jobs must we fill in the classroom? Which one do you want to be first?
- ✓ Where are homework assignments listed?
- ✓ What one thing in the classroom makes you go hmmmm?
- ✓ Where can I find out what's for lunch?
- ✓ Where would you find the supply drawer of paper?
- ✓ What is the back bulletin board about?
- ✓ How will we decide who sits in the bean bags?
- ✓ Where will you put notes from home?
- ✓ Where are the staplers and tape located?
- ✓ What table number are you sitting at? Find the corresponding bookshelf; place your reading book there.
- ✓ Where is the pencil sharpener located?

Morning Greeting

Introduce a greeting ritual to help your students get to know one another and become more comfortable with each other. This also helps to reinforce the feeling of belonging. For the first few weeks, you'll need to lead the greeting, demonstrating how to greet classmates appropriately—look them in the eye and shake hands. Some students may feel uncomfortable with the process at first, so make light of it. You can jokingly demonstrate how not to greet someone, demonstrating a creepy stare, an untrustworthy glance, or a mushy handshake. You might also say, "Some of you are very strong—and, as you know, with great power comes great responsibility—so please don't crush people's fingers!"

Start with a basic handshake and saying "Hello" to about five people. Eventually, you can hand over the lead to a student, who gets to choose how many people the class will greet that morning. Always participate yourself, to continue modeling correct behavior. Over time, to keep this ritual interesting, introduce a new handshake and greeting option:

Shake	*Greeting*
Knuckle punch	Good morning/afternoon!
High/low 5	Welcome back!
High/low 10	Glad you're here!
Up high, down low	What's up?
Pinky shake	Buenos dias
Mini-five	Howdy!
Foot shake	Greetings!
Behind the back	Hi there!

Classroom Snapshot

Every morning, my student, Dan, goes to the office to give the announcements over the loudspeaker, so he often arrives in the middle of our morning greeting. At the beginning of the year, when he tried to sneak back into the room unnoticed, I proclaimed, *Let's get Dan! He's back! We ALL need to give him a greeting!* With much laughter, Dan was bombarded by his classmates giving him a high five.

Now, months later, students complete their required greetings and wait by the door for Dan to come back from the office. What a great feeling he must get when he arrives back at the room and finds a barrage of friends making a point to wait and greet him every day.

Get to Know You

Students won't take risks until they feel comfortable with their classmates. Over the first few weeks, use some of the following games and questionnaires to help your students gradually get to know each other in a risk free, fun environment.

2 Truths and a Lie

On an index card, each student and the teacher create two obscure truths about themselves as well as one realistic lie. To share, individuals read their list, and the rest of the class tries to decide are the truths and which is the lie. The funny thing about this activity is that the students often struggle with creating a lie!

Find A Friend Who . . .

Give your students a Find A Friend Who . . . form (see below a form created for 5th and 6th grade students) and ask them to fill in the blanks on any square that has an asterisk (*). Then challenge them to find a friend who matches the description in each one of their boxes. When they find someone, that person signs the box. Before they start, explain that if the answer to their first question is no, they shouldn't give up on that student, but keep on asking questions—surely they will match with one of the boxes! Also, challenge them to try to get a different signature in every box—meaning, once they get a yes, they should thank that person and find someone else to ask.

Find a friend who . . .			
. . . loves vanilla ice cream.	. . . is wearing the same size of shoe as you.*	. . . has seen the movie *Charlie and the Chocolate Factory.*	. . . owns a bicycle and a helmet.
. . . has more than five letters in their name.	. . . is the youngest in the family.	. . . likes to eat Chinese food.	. . . loves the same color as you.*
. . . loves your favorite animal.*	. . . knows how to play a musical instrument.	. . . has the same birthday month as you.*	. . . has traveled to another country.
. . . likes to go camping	. . . has more than two siblings.	. . . is ten years old.	. . . loves to draw.
. . . read at least four books over vacation.	. . . likes to swim.	. . . brought his/her lunch to school today.	. . . can count to ten in a foreign language. (Listen to them do it!)

Rituals

Finally, we can build trust by supporting our students with a strong culture, built on familiar rituals and explicit expectations of behavior. Routines and rituals establish a sense of calm, peace, and low stress. Outside school, many students' lives are hectic, unstructured, and unpredictable. Knowing what to expect when they walk through the threshold of your classroom is often a relief.

Classroom Snapshot

One morning Laura walked into the class and, out of the blue, talking to no one in particular, she said, *Ahhh, this place… this place… it just makes me feel calm, relaxed, and peaceful!* When I asked her what she meant by that she said, grinning ear to ear, *I don't know. I just love walking into this room.*

Rituals are a vital part of strengthening social bonds, and they exist whether we create them or not. The key is to deliberately create helpful rituals that support the learning process and sustain trust between all parties. After a few weeks, your classroom should be run by simple, automatic routines and rituals. This will allow you to stop shouting and organizing and stand back and observe, support, and guide your students; it will put your focus on students—not on managing behavior. While routines take time to set up, this is a rewarding investment in creating an efficient and self-sufficient classroom for the rest of the year. Once you've set them up, all you need to do is trigger the routine or ritual and sit back.

Classroom Snapshot

Our class had just started correcting our daily work when I was pulled out into the hallway for about five minutes. In my absence, the class finished the piece we were correcting when I stepped out. Next, one student had stepped up, counted everyone off to complete the short answer problems on another piece of work. By the time I returned, each team was quietly discussing the essay question at the bottom of the page. It was as if I hadn't even stepped out of the room!

Every classroom activity can be established as a routine. Here are some ideas to get you started, together with tips for setting up routines and rituals in the first few weeks:

- Music for transitions
- Strong morning rituals
- Celebrate learning
- Meet in the middle

Music for Transitions

You can use musical triggers to define and control the entire school day. Choose a specific song for each major component of your day, including regular class activities.

For example:

Activity	*Trigger Song Ideas*	*Artist*
Get ready for the day/ lesson	"Good Morning Starshine" "Here Comes the Sun" "The Sound of Sunshine"	Oliver Beatles (from the musical)
Recess	"Get Ready for This"	2 Unlimited
Lunch	"Yummy, Yummy, Yummy"	Ohio Express
Grab your detective jackets; we have a new "case" to solve	Theme from *CSI:* "Who Are You?"	The Who
Pair up for a one minute read	"Sing, Sing, Sing"	*Chicago* (the musical)
Time to do our end of the day jobs for dismissal	"Takin' Care of Business"	Bachman-Turner Overdrive

Once the songs are established, you don't have to expend any effort to transition your students from one activity to another—except to push *play*. The music does the rest of the work for you, launching your students into the next activity.

Beginning Song

While most of these songs stay the same for the whole year, if you want to, you can rotate your beginning song every few weeks, as this is the first song of the day. Or, have a standard song, but mix in topical tunes to reflect the Olympics, Valentine's Day, or the start of summer. Whatever your theme, choose upbeat, cheery songs to announce the start of your lesson.

Your beginning song is a signal to your students that you will be starting soon. The idea is, by the end of the song, students need to have all the supplies they're going to need for the day or lesson, and (perhaps) their homework out so you can check it together after the song is over. As soon as they hear the opening bars, your students should automatically pick up the pace and get ready.

To establish this ritual or routine, simply talk your students through the process whenever you play the song for the first few weeks. So, it might work like this:

Start your song—pause it.

That's this week's starting song.

Play five seconds more—pause it.

Do you have all the books you need?

Play ten seconds more—pause it.

Do you have your homework out?

Play one minute more—pause it.

Will you be ready by the time the song ends?

Play the rest of the song.

It's very important that you are ready to begin when the song ends, or it defeats the purpose of the song. Never start the song until *you* are ready to start!

Even after the first few weeks, you'll need to keep reinforcing the behavior you expect. When the designated song has played for fifteen seconds, pause it and gently remind your students, "This is our starting song . . . Make sure you have your materials, and your homework is out and ready to correct." Eventually, once the ritual is established, your students will no longer need the reminder. You'll probably find they start getting organized and ready even before the song is complete. At that point, you can joke with them and say, "Bonus points for singing along!"

Very occasionally—often close to vacations—the starting song will suddenly fail to produce the required activity in certain students. All you have to do is a quick sweep of the room, making positive comments about those who are organized and ready to go. "Nice going Jacob, you have all your materials out and ready." "This team is on top of things, they have all their supplies gathered." The stragglers immediately leap into action, and the ritual is restored.

Classroom Snapshot

My students still talk about "the day the music died"—when I left my iPod at home. The day was just way TOO quiet!!

Mingle and Move Music. Music is also extremely useful as a trigger to move. Use music whenever you want students to get into partnerships or teams, or simply transition to the next activity. Establish early on that your students can't mingle or move until the music begins. Here's how to set this up:

Teacher: "Please stand up!" PAUSE "When the music begins ... WHEN?"

Students: "When the music begins!"

Teacher: "Move to the next activity station."

Music plays . . .

Background music

It's helpful to use music in the background, whenever your students are working on projects, playing games, or even taking tests. Very occasionally, students are bothered by music during a test, but most prefer it to the drop dead silence of the test room. For most students, gentle, reflective music calms nervous students, as well as buffering any extraneous sounds coming from next door, the hallway, or fellow students flipping through pages. In addition, slower working students are glad to have the music drowned out sounds from other students, which would normally make them anxious that they are the only ones still writing and everyone else has finished. Under the cover of music, slower students can't hear people closing up their books or rustling materials. The music seems to lull them into a test taking trance. If some of your students don't like background music, get them used to it slowly by playing very quiet music, with no lyrics, during quiet working time.

Last year my class had started a test and the music wasn't playing. I was looking at the test and trying to answer the questions, but without the music I couldn't answer any of the questions. So I quietly asked Mrs. Currie to turn on the music and then my brain power started pumping.

—Elizabeth May, middle school student

At the other end of the spectrum, when students are working on projects where they are cutting and pasting, upbeat music will help them to be more productive. Cardio mixes are excellent at keeping students moving in their pasting process—rather than the leisurely pace they tend to adopt if left to their own devices.

Where to Find Music

If you'd like to try using thematic music—songs with lyrics that match the lesson—consider checking out *The Green Book of Songs*. This amazing resource will give you numerous ideas for songs that might have a lyrical match to your lesson. This information is available in book format or online at greenbookofsongs.com.

In addition, for background music, try www.reflectioncd.com, which allows you to download an album onto your computer. They carry a wide variety of reflective and relaxation music. You can also find inexpensive relaxation and workout CDs in the major chain stores.

Classroom Snapshot

Once I started using routines, it all came together. It was less of me and more of them. There was ownership—not *my* classroom, but *ours*. When the students can run the classroom, you know that the routines are working. There are actually times when I leave school feeling guilty because it seems like I just sat back and watched. —Chris Straub, 4th grade teacher, Commodore Perry School District

Strong Morning Rituals

To help your students feel at home in your classroom, make sure they know what's expected of them as soon as they walk in the room (Allen, 2010, p. 131). Establish some activities that students complete by themselves before class starts officially. Here are some ideas to add to your classroom:

- Sign-in
- Read the message board
- Gather materials
- Check-in with the teacher
- Prework
- TRANSITION: Beginning song

Sign-In

To get your students into the right frame of mind as they enter your classroom, welcome them with a novel way of signing-in:

- *Tally Tag*—Put two options on the board for the students to choose between and place their vote. Choices could be as simple as: Chocolate/Vanilla; Warm/Cold; Red/Orange; Pizza/French Fries; or Summer/Winter. Or let the first student into the room come up with the options for that morning.
- *One Question*—Create a sign-in activity on the board. As students come in and check in, they each have to add a punctuation mark to a piece of unedited text, or answer an easy question for review. You want the activity to be low-risk, so the students succeed with their first act of the day.
- *Lucky Dip*—students draw a part-of-speech card out of a bucket. They stick their card on the board (with a magnet or blue tack), write a sentence beside it, underline the part of the sentence they drew (e.g., adjective), and initial their work before heading to their seats.

Activities like this ensure students start thinking as soon as they step into your classroom. The sign-in activity draws their attention away from any issues that may have occurred prior to class, engaging them immediately.

Read the Message Board

Keep a designated board in the back of your classroom for messages. These are simply daily reminders of the work for today, upcoming due dates, and changes in the daily schedule. As soon as students have signed in, they go directly to that board to find information on assemblies, visitors, shortened time frames, or change in start time.

Gather Materials

Each day, use this board to list the materials your students will need. This way, students come in, check the board for needed supplies, gather them, and get themselves organized in a minimal amount of time, before class actually starts.

Check-In With the Teacher

While your students are gathering materials, set yourself up in a designated part of the classroom for check-in. This can be your desk, if you have one, or another table or supplies cart. This is the signal for students who have gathered their supplies to bring up their homework for a twenty-second check-in. For many teachers, this becomes a favorite part of the day; you have a chance to greet students individually, ask them how they are, inquire about their current novel, and scan their homework for any glaring misunderstandings. Usefully, students will often tell you where they had difficulty the night before.

Use the check-in to congratulate students on work well done or privately catch academic issues before they become large problems. Quickly scan the homework and provide immediate feedback—Is it neat? Complete? Restated? If not, hand it back with constructive comments and give your students a chance to fix their errors. Where work is of high quality, use the opportunity to make a big deal over neat, well written, or creative work. This is not just for the benefit of the student you're talking to. Others will hear your comments and lock them away for future reference. This process shows your students that you care about what work they are doing and how they are doing it. It helps to keep expectations high.

Prework

To keep students busy during check-in, and get their brains in gear, set a quick five-minute activity of *prework* tied into your curriculum. Daily language/math reviews from Carson Dellosa are very useful, giving a quick preview/review.

Celebrate Learning!

Learning something new is a huge accomplishment and it needs to be celebrated! Celebrations bring joy and excitement into the classroom, giving your students a sense of pride and feelings of success. Early on, establish team cheers, clapping sequences, or shout outs for the class to celebrate individual student or group achievements when learning goals are accomplished. Spend some time teaching and modeling these cheers, so your class becomes comfortable with them. Here are some examples:

Teacher:	"Great answer Blake! Everyone give him two claps."
Class:	CLAP, CLAP (Or another option is two stomps)
Teacher:	"Well said Laura! Give her a BOOM, BOOM!"
Class:	"BOOM, BOOM, FIRE POWER!"
Teacher:	"Great detail in your explanation John. He deserves a SOUP-er cheer!"
Class:	(pretends they are using a can opener to open a can of soup, sniffs and says) "Mmmmm, Mmmmm, Good!"

Meet in the Middle

Establish a general meeting area in your room where the class convenes for various activities—to discuss classroom issues, share an artifact, update your daily schedule, listen to a book talk, or assemble for teambuilding activities. Depending on the size of your class, the meeting place can be in the front of the room around a rug, or in the middle of the room where students can easily turn their chairs or desks to form a giant circle. Bringing the whole class together in one, large, unified circle conveys an important message: *We are a community; everyone is included.*

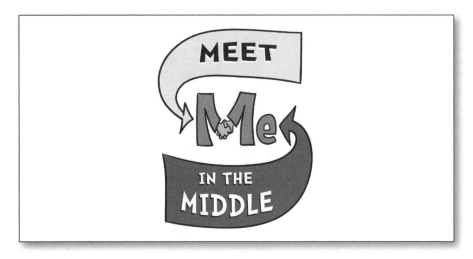

You'll probably use this meeting area at least once per class period, so it's important to get the class there quickly and in an organized fashion. You want to make sure students bring all the materials they will need, rather than having them run back for missing items.

Here are the instructional steps for this routine:

1. Teacher: "Please stand up!" Wait . . . "Push in your chair." Wait until all students are standing and facing you.

2. Teacher "You will need THREE things." (holding up 3 fingers) "How many?"

3. Students: "THREE!"

4. Teacher: "In just a moment, you will need to gather your reading book, case file, and tool kit. What three things?"

5. Students: "Reading book, case file, and tool kit!"

6. Teacher: "Great! 1, 2, what do you do?"

7. Students: "3, 4, hit the floor!"

While establishing this *meeting in the middle* routine, you'll find a few students, especially the shy, uncertain ones, who will try to stay on the fringes of the circle. Make sure you explicitly ask students to move so everyone is included. Also, give students the option to sit on the floor or on their chairs, as long as the class forms a recognizable circle or oval and *all* members are included. This is a key moment, when your class comes together, so it is important students feel as comfortable as possible.

Key Points

- Trust is the safety net that will allow your students to run the risk of failure.
- Yet, by middle school, many students have stopped trusting their teachers.
- Mistakes are good—we cannot learn without them—our student must feel comfortable to make mistakes, without fear of punishment or ridicule.
- Stop saying *No!* Start asking *Why?*
- Make your classroom a safe learning environment.
- Allow your students to own the space.
- Introduce predictable routines to drive your classroom activities.

3

Create a Collaborative Community

An enormous part of being successful in life requires that we play well with others. In one form or another, we need to be able to interact successfully with our friends and family, peers, and coworkers. One of our most critical life skills is the ability to communicate, work, and negotiate with other people. Given students' growing ability to articulate their thoughts and feelings, and their increased levels of social awareness, the middle school classroom is the perfect place where this central life skill can be nurtured, honed, and refined.

Yet, this is rarely the case. As students exit the typically collaborative years of their elementary education and enter the middle years, there seems to be a counter-intuitive shift toward expecting them succeed primarily as *individuals*. Certainly, eventually, they must be able to accomplish tasks on their own. However, for most middle school students, having the assistance of their peers as they learn to do this both accelerates this process and helps them achieve at a higher level, while simultaneously developing their interpersonal skills.

Why Collaborative Learning Improves Educational Outcomes

The brain can only take in so much information before it overloads itself and begins to overwrite the given information. When we give students new ideas, it's the equivalent of piling papers onto their desk. If we keep talking, it doesn't take long before the pile of paper (ideas) gets too big and slides onto the floor (is lost from the student's short-term memory)—becoming lost forever (forgotten). If we want students to hang onto these papers (ideas), we must give them time to sort and organize them, and put them safely in a filing cabinet (long-term memory), along with similar papers (ideas) where they can easily retrieve (remember) them. The point is, students do not learn when you pile paper on their desks, they only learn when you direct them to pick up the papers and manipulate them by sorting, organizing, and filing. It is this manipulation that creates meaning.

Collaborative learning is so powerful, because it requires students to *share* their ideas with someone else—a partner or a group—which, in turn, makes them *perform* this act of manipulation by thinking about the idea first. In effect, it allows them to bite, chew, and digest ideas. The process of sharing also allows students to gather new perspectives from fellow students, clear up misunderstandings, and eventually put this new and improved information back into their memories. This is why:

Those who talk the most learn the most.

Allowing your students to talk about what you just told them makes them take the information, roll it around in their mind, and make sense of the material. As students discuss what they do and don't understand, a huge amount of manipulation goes on their brains, laying down long-term memories. Thus, those who talk most about a topic are also likely to be those who understand and remember it best.

Additional Benefits of Collaborative Learning

If we encourage students to succeed together, learning through discussion and dialogue, this refines their understanding of the topic. Often, it's a student explanation that creates the brightest spark of understanding with a peer. A stronger student can help guide another student through the learning process using "kid language," while themselves gaining a deeper understanding of the material through what for them is a review process.

Also, working alone, students will only focus on their own opinions, perceptions, and values—which narrows their thinking. Isolated opinions, whether right or wrong, rapidly harden into concrete belief. Lacking external input, beliefs become mentally set in stone and extremely difficult to change. By contrast, working together helps to create a more flexible and diverse way of thinking. Students who are able to toss ideas back and forth, express opinions, gradually form a more complex outlook on a topic. In effect, having a partner or two increases the amount of paper we can manipulate and ultimately store into our filing cabinets.

Through this process, students also learn to respect and value each other's different strengths, styles, and thinking. Their potentially narrow, individual views blossom into broader, more carefully thought out ideas. This ability to gain a diverse understanding of an idea—built on the input of multiple sources—is the foundation of critical thinking.

Collaborative learning is also a lifesaver for students who lack confidence (Fisher & Frey, 2008, p. 36). When they hear others' ideas, these students start to realize they have similar thoughts—helping them understand they too have something to contribute. As their confidence grows, they begin to participate more. The more they participate, the more they learn, and suddenly a child who has never before achieved at school discovers they *can* learn—often a literally life-changing moment.

For all students, learning collaboratively helps them to appreciate the perspectives of and to work and communicate effectively with others—all critical social skills. If students don't learn social skills in their middle years, they will be woefully unprepared for high school, where social interaction dominates their development on all levels. It is not a biological accident that friends and peers become the focus of teenage life. Social skills are needed to thrive as an adult. And, as most high school teachers know, concern for subject matter tends to take a distant back seat to students' interest in each other. Therefore, the better we, as middle school teachers, can prepare students to succeed collaboratively, the better prepared they will be to not only successfully interact with their peers, but to save at least some of their focus for high school content, when it comes time to learn.

Collaborate and Cooperate—or *Compete?*

The argument against collaborative learning is that students must learn to compete with their peers to be successful in life. After all, the thinking goes, the real world is filled with competition—for superior jobs, for higher raises, for better spouses! Those who compete successfully will go the furthest, as they race past their slower-moving peers. It then follows that the sooner the educational process allows students to compete against one another, the sooner they will develop these critical life skills, and thus be better prepared to succeed.

The problem with this view of life in general—and education in particular—is that, while we often see competition as a natural part of life (survival of the fittest), our societies and economies depend on people working together for the common good. This has always been the case. Our human ancestors participated in family groups, gathering groups, hunting groups, raiding groups, and so on. Almost everything was done in a social context; to be alone was to be in danger. As a species, we learned that individual success is not always desirable if it occurs at the expense of the group.

We do our students a disservice if we let them believe that all situations are inherently competitive. If we foster individual competitiveness at the middle school level, we create citizens who enter every situation looking for what they need to do to succeed, who their enemies are, and how to win. On the other hand, if we give students an early understanding of the benefits that can be derived from working together with others, they will be able to make a proactive choice:

Is this a situation that requires a group approach, or is this a time when competition is actually the healthy choice for everyone?

To be successful human beings, students need to understand the difference between these two choices. Consistently facing life from a competitive vantage point will certainly generate some accomplishments, victories, and triumphs. However, it also comes with the enormous cost of missed opportunities. Often, cooperation creates greater success than would ever have been possible with one individual striving vigorously to be "King of the Mountain."

Cooperation Must Be Taught

As teachers, we must be aware that:

Competition is learned naturally, while cooperation must be taught.

Without guidance from their teacher, middle school students will not embark on a journey of personal development that recognizes the value of cooperation. Left to their own devices, they will instinctively become increasingly competitive with each other. They will compare scores, reports, and feedback within the classroom environment—just as they do in the sporting arena. We don't need to teach our students about winners and losers, champion and chumps. The playground and the media do that for them. However, we do need to teach them that there is more to life than winning and about the skills they need for successful cooperation.

A group working together successfully requires individuals with a multitude of social skills, as well as a high level of interpersonal awareness. While some students inherently bring a natural understanding of these skills with them, they are always in the minority. To bring cooperation between peers into your classroom, you need to teach these skills consciously and carefully, and nurture them continuously throughout the middle school years.

Fortunately, in the middle school classroom, almost every interaction is a chance to further students' understanding of the concept of cooperation and mutual support. Whether it be small group activities or large classroom events, or whether in interactions between peers or interactions between student and teacher—within all these moments, opportunities abound to model, demonstrate, and elaborate to students how helping each other can lead to a higher level of achievement by all. This chapter isolates, highlights, and identifies many of these key moments and provides specific strategies for handling them in a way that furthers the learning process.

Teachers who deliberately develop peer cooperation at the middle school levels are preparing students to truly succeed in life. This is the ultimate teaching moment—a chance to influence lives by teaching skills that will open doors to new opportunities and improve their quality of life for years to come.

How to Create a Collaborative Community

In a collaborative classroom, students first listen, then work the material, talk about the material, work again with the material, and finally file the material for future use. In most classrooms, this requires three critical changes:

1. Make the physical environment conducive to collaboration

2. Create multiple opportunities for students to talk about new information

3. Use deliberate memory strategies to help students retrieve the information they eventually file away

Make the Physical Environment Conducive to Collaboration

In a collaborative classroom, teachers don't stand at the front of the room, hand out work sheets, and return to their desks. Students don't have desks and don't sit in rows. The entire classroom becomes an interactive teaching tool—including the floor and the ceiling— where students are encouraged to touch, get involved, and take ownership of their learning environment.

Ditch Your Desk

If your students do most of the talking, your role as a teacher necessarily changes. You will spend less time talking from the front and more time in the trenches with your students, guiding from the sidelines and facilitating feedback. This means you will no longer be anchored to your desk. Instead, you will be moving around, listening in to conversations, guiding students back on track, and answering their questions. You'll get to hear students reach their *Aha!* moments and quickly realize their misconceptions—invaluable insights to inform your teaching.

Since your desk takes up valuable teaching space—and you're no longer going to be behind it—you may as well get rid of it. If you keep your desk, it will create a barrier between you and your students. It says, *I am the teacher, and you are the student.* If you're really going to create a collaborative classroom, you must be part of the room and available for collaboration and consultation. So, your desk goes. This is a great opportunity to throw out all the useless odds and ends you've accumulated over the years. Of course, you'll still need some storage space for your essential teaching items. A rolling AV cart is ideal so you can take your supplies where you need them.

Use Round Tables, Not Rows of Desks

Throw out your desks and replace them with round tables. Rows of desks are unproductive seating arrangements. Not only do they inhibit collaboration, passing materials back through rows sucks up spare seconds. With tables, papers and material can quickly be tossed into the center and distributed in a fleeting moment. Also, you want to avoid a desk becoming a student's territory. In a collaborative classroom, students move around and work in different places. Every*thing* in the room belongs to every*one* in the room.

Round tables lend themselves better to conversation, because they let each student see each other while speaking and sharing or listening to his teammates. By contrast, rectangular or square tables can create a sense of hierarchy—or the opportunity to have a face off—which is exactly what you want to avoid. This is the time middle schoolers are trying to find their pecking order. With round tables, everyone is on equal ground, at least as far as their seating positions go.

Community Supplies

One of the simplest ways to create a sense of community is to set up your classroom for sharing. This starts with supplies. Keep a set of supplies in a central, easy accessible location and encourage your students to help themselves without asking. Aim to have a counter and many of your cupboards designated specifically for students. To keep things neat, it's worth placing labels to indicate where things need to be put back and the contents of drawers. Place cups filled with pencils around the room—you can fill them with the pencils that are found on the floor at the end of each day. Tell your students, if they need a pencil, they can simply go to a pencil cup and grab one.

Don't worry about your students getting greedy and hoarding supplies. Once they realize there is a supply readily available, students start to use community supplies respectfully and become quickly willing to share.

DO Touch

In a collaborative classroom, everything can be touched. Classrooms are not display homes. You want your students to dive into learning, not loiter uncertainly on the edges. Because many classrooms are *Do Not Touch* zones, students are often reluctant to be hands on at first. You'll have to proactively tell them, "You can touch anything you like. If it's in this classroom, it's there for you."

Just as your students should talk more than you, so they should also touch more than you do. For example, if you have an interactive whiteboard in your room, your students should be the primary people interacting with it.

Classroom Snapshot

Many years ago, a retiring colleague gave me a huge box of seashells, starfish, and coral—a true treasure chest. The items were so beautiful and fragile, I hesitated to let my students touch them. But then I heard my students say they had never seen the ocean or touched a seashell before in their life. And so I handed out my treasure to an enthralled classroom. I will never forget their faces and their excited conversations—or how much they remembered from that day. From that point on, I made sure my classroom was a *DO TOUCH* classroom, where everyone got to experience their learning hands-on.

Meeting Area

Using tables gives you more space in the classroom, allowing you to create a general meeting area. This is just a space, generally distinguished with a rug, where your class meets together as a whole group. You might introduce your daily objective here. Try to keep your meeting area close to the front of the room so you can access the board.

Whenever you call a meeting, let your students choose whether they sit comfortably on the rug, slide a chair up to sit on, or lie on the floor. However, make sure you can see everyone's eyeballs and they are ALL in the circle. Make it a big deal that no one is permitted to sit outside the circle.

Alternative Seating

When partners or groups go off to complete an activity, let them choose where they work. If you have space, provide some alternative seating options throughout your classroom. For example, you might have beanbags, or a wooden storage trunk, or a small couch, or a wooden table with stools. Students may also choose the rug, the back counter, the floor, and of course, the various tables teams use daily. The only restriction you need to enforce is that partnerships must be on the same level. Meaning, if a partner is sitting in a chair, both need to be in chairs. If one is on the floor, both need to be on the floor. Conversations are more productive when students are at eye level with each other.

Using Every Inch of Space as "Teaching Space"

Every aspect of your classroom—its walls, floor, ceiling, even its airwaves—has a teaching purpose.

Walls "Under Construction"

Resist the urge to fill the walls with worthy educational posters before your students arrive on the first day. Instead, other than a few motivational posters, put caution tape and *Walls under construction ~ Work coming soon!* signs across your bulletin boards. You're going to use your walls to teach, so they need to be built with your students, around what you are currently learning. As you progress through the year, you will continue to add new elements to them.

Try to design what ends up on your walls with your students— rather than use ready-made posters. As you learn new concepts, ask your students to create posters or sayings as memory aids. Encourage your students to *use the walls* while working; for example, if they are stuck on a problem, encourage them to walk around and remind themselves from the memory aids and explanations on the walls. New knowledge is often in rough draft form—meaning, when information is newly learned, it's not there permanently until practiced a good amount of times. So, having information located on the walls for reference will help your students to solidify that information at their own pace and in their own way.

By the end of the year, the walls will serve as a continual review. Because your students helped build the walls, they will know where each piece of information is located and remember the moment they created it. When it's test time, even though the information will now be covered, many students will be able to retrieve the information by looking at the spot where the information used to be displayed. This is called *memory by location* (see below).

Your students will also enjoy seeing the progress and reflecting on the huge amount of information they have learned throughout the year. At a glance, they can proudly see how much they have mastered.

Whiteboards (on the walls)

If possible, put whiteboards on several walls. This gives you opportunities to teach from many sides of the room. It also means you can use location to help students grasp ideas that need distinct awareness. For example, if you're learning about three different triangles, put each on a different board. Then, if a student gets stuck, you can point and say, "Remember a few days ago when we were talking about the three triangles? The triangle you're looking at was on *this* whiteboard. What was it called again?"

Floor Space

The floor is the most underutilized space in the classroom. You can use it to create teaching infrastructure by laying down giant number grids (jump those times tables!) or giant keyboards (hop those spelling words!). When tables are too small to hold all the materials for an activity—move to the floor! And the floor is the ideal prop to learn about area and perimeters.

You can also use it as a giant memory aid. Get your students to cut out giant, multi-colored feet (a Shaquille O'Neal size 20 is ideal), and write reminders on them. For example, you might include formulas for circumference, definitions of various terms, character traits, and anything else your students think are important, yet hard to remember. If possible, secure them to the floor using contact paper so you effectively have Shaq's feet walking into and around your room. Put the footprints in high traffic areas, and anywhere else students tend to sit or congregate. Then, if their attention happens to fade during instruction time, they can at least tune into something useful by reading the floor or walls. You can make review more fun by asking your students to take a walk. Play music while the students follow the feet until the music stops. They find a foot closest to them, read it, and share its message with their closest neighbor.

If you aren't allowed to adhere things to your floor, or if you want to use this technique for a specific topic, use index cards instead. Get your students to write down vocabulary, spelling words, or numbers on index cards and scatter them across the floor and around the tables. Then, ask students to walk around and find a word matching a given definition, or possibly stand on a word/problem and solve it.

Mini-Whiteboards

Mini-whiteboards, or mini-boards, help to keep your students engaged when a peer is working on one of the main boards. If your school doesn't have them, use old chalk board squares, or place cardstock inside sheet protectors, which work fine with dry erase markers. Whenever someone comes up to try a problem, every student sitting watching should be doing the same problem on their mini-board.

You can also use them for quick visual assessment. In this case, you pose a question, and students respond on their whiteboards. Then, when most students are done, give the signal: *1, 2, 3, SHOOT!* And all students hold their boards up to face you. This means you can do an extremely quick visual check for understanding, and quickly give corrective feedback where necessary. If all is well, you can move on to the next problem.

Using the Airwaves

The airwaves in a collaborative classroom are alive with music! From the time the students walk through your door, to the time they leave, music should play almost all day. In Chapter 2, we talked about using music a cue and in the background. Another important use is as a sound pad whenever students are talking in partners or small groups. For example, if you say, "Talk to your partner. Why do you think the hero was embarrassed when the teacher read out his poem?" immediately play music. Otherwise, you get deadly silence, and no student wants to be the first one to break it—because everyone will be listening! But if music is already playing, even shy students will feel comfortable talking under its cover. Music also makes it less likely that a conversation from one group will disturb another.

Don't worry about the volume level. Using music while students are collaborating actually helps keep the noise level to a minimum. The music acts as the volume barrier. If you want to take down the volume in your room—simply turn down the music and the voices will naturally follow.

Music also sets the tone in your classroom. Playing fun, fast-paced popular hits—"Funkytown," "I Like to Move It," We Like to Party," and "(I've Got) The Power," gets students motivated and moving. On the other hand, if it's an unusual day—with an excursion or school pictures—where you know students will be walking in already pumped up—opt for calm, soothing music to help settle their excitement. You might choose contemporary music selections from William Ackerman, Yanni, Kenny G, or from the many *Lifescapes* collections.

Ceiling

Don't forget the ceiling. Extending a clothesline across the room from end to end gives you additional space to hang up information or work. You can use clothespins to hang posters, murals, and memory aids. Where appropriate, hang items in a logical order to help students remember the information in that location, and then stand under that spot when you're talking about the information.

Library

If you have room, section off a portion of your classroom as a library. Deck it out with beanbags, a rug, and a lamp so students can relax as they read. As well as your school's reading curriculum, dedicate some shelves to your class's favorite authors and keep a shelf or basket of *Red Hot Reads*. These are novels that come highly recommended by students or you.

Create Multiple Opportunities for Students to Talk About Information

Pairing/Sharing

To keep your students learning, find constant opportunities to let them pair up, share what they know, or work together to better solidify the current topic. After some initial instruction, you can use paired discussions (Marzano & Pickering, 2011, p. 71), paired timed tests, paired work to solve specific problems, partner-based activities, paired development of memory aids—the list goes on and on. The idea is that students will rarely work alone while they're still mastering a concept. This approach helps to eliminate behavior problems by keeping students engaged and happy, because students like to talk.

Find a way of assigning pairs at random. Ask each student to write their name on a Popsicle stick and draw names. If you're concerned about two learning-support students being drawn together, it's easy to inconspicuously ensure this never happens. On the other hand, sometimes having these students paired up can be an advantage—as you can spend more time with these pairs.

Clearly, with this random method, students will sometimes be paired with people they don't know or don't like. Getting on with people you don't care for is an important life skill, so don't give in to the groans. In fact, it's a good idea to address this issue head on, before your first pairing activity. With the group sitting together in your meeting area, explain that you are going do a ton of paired work throughout the year, and that eventually they will be working with everyone, multiple times. And, yes, this means they might have to work with someone they don't particularly like. But before they go, "Oh yuck!" they should consider how they would feel if they were on the other end of the "Oh yuck!" moment. You might want to point out that, when we pair up, we aren't *marrying* the person. It's simply a partnership that lasts fifteen minutes. Some lessons, they might have two or three different partners. These aren't long-term commitments!

A good strategy to avoid the mix-and-match groans is to insist that when you call out the pairs, they have to look at each other, wave their biggest wave, and smile a big toothy grin. You'll have to do this with them, waving at each and every pair, with your own toothy grin. It means each paired activity starts with a laugh, and cuts through the stress.

Eventually, you'll notice that even the most reluctant students get used to working with different people. It's an excellent lesson in tolerance and flexibility—as well as being a massive support for the learning process.

Classroom Snapshot

One year, I noticed my students weren't as comfortable with each other as in past years, and I couldn't figure out why. I had been doing team-building activities, table-team activities, and yet the cohesiveness still wasn't there. Students I'd had the previous year commented: *We just don't feel like a big family like last year.* It finally dawned on me—we weren't pairing up as often.

So, I took a hard look at my program and purposely designed activities that allowed partner work at least once per day. It didn't take long to see the transformation take place. Once we started mixing and mingling more, the students became more comfortable with each other. They took more risks in their learning and became more open and tolerant with each other.

Courteous Conversations

If your students are going to learn through discussions, they need to acquire some rudimentary skills about conversing courteously. This starts with learning not to be derogatory when a fellow student says something they disagree with. An ideal place to teach this basic skill is when the class corrects homework orally. Before you do this for the first time, discuss with your students that laughing, pulling faces, and yelling out "Huh? I didn't get that!" is inappropriate. Instead, ask them to say, "I think there's a better answer."

Then you can practice by going through the homework answers. Whenever they are challenged in this way, offer the answering student a moment to look back into the homework to see if she can correct the mistake. If she cannot, she can simply call S.O.S. and ask a friend to give the correct answer for her. To hold the incorrect student accountable, return to her at the end, making sure she's jotted down the correct answer, and then ask her to repeat it. So it might work like this:

Lindsey:	"Number two, the synonym for *good* is *bad*."
Class:	"I think there's a better answer."
Lindsey:	(Takes a moment to reevaluate her answer.) "Oh, I see where I made my mistake. I thought it was the opposite. The synonym for *good* is *well-behaved*."
Class:	"I agree!"

OR

Lindsey:	"Number two, the synonym for *good* is *bad*."
Class:	"I think there's a better answer."
Lindsey:	(Takes a moment to reevaluate her answer.) "I just don't see where I made my mistake." Hands are waving all over the place to help her out. "S.O.S Shelby."
Shelby:	"The synonym for *good* is *well-behaved*."
Class:	"I agree!"
Lindsey:	"Oh, now I get it. I thought it was an opposite!"
Teacher:	"OK, Lindsey, what's the correct answer?"
Lindsey:	The synonym for *good* is *well-behaved*."

Teacher and Class:	"Nice job!" "Good try, Lindsey." "High five, Lindsey."
Lindsey:	"Thanks, Shelby."

This process, although extremely simple, is a vital part of empowering shy or less able students to have a go. You'll find student participation at an all-time high, if you give them a chance to redeem themselves and provide a safety net if they can't figure out the answer. By contrast, if you dismiss a wrong answer and just move on, the deflated and embarrassed student will not want to participate the next time. If you take the lead in this, always encouraging the act of simply having a go, you'll soon see your students supporting and complimenting each other.

Classroom Snapshot

When students feel safe to get things wrong, they also gain confidence in their own thinking. For example, one day when Cameron was providing the answer, most of the class disagreed with her. Here's what it sounded like:

Cameron:	The answer to 3 is B.
Class:	I think there's a better answer!
Cameron:	(Takes a few seconds to reevaluate her response.) I think I'm right. I have the evidence right here from the article. (She reads her evidence).

Natalie is waving her hand vigorously.

Teacher:	Natalie, do you agree or disagree with Cameron?
Natalie:	I agree, and I have additional evidence that supports her answer. (She reads her evidence).

At this point, I confirmed that Cameron's *B* was in fact the correct answer. The point is, although the majority of the class disagreed with Cameron, she stuck to her guns and stayed with her evidence.

You'll also have to teach your students how to ask questions politely. For example, if a student mumbles an answer, rather than chorusing, "WHAT?" ask him to say, "Could you please repeat that? I didn't hear it properly." This isn't rocket science, but these tiny courtesies are essential to productive conversations, as well as making a huge impact on behavior, emotions, and the entire climate of the classroom.

Give Me the Hard Cold Facts

Your students also need to learn how to refute answers they disagree with. Tell them, you always need *why*—you want hard cold facts—perhaps based on the text or reminding the class of a definition or a method, to rebut the given answer. To get this point across in a fun way, give each student a pair of cheap sunglasses. When a student wants to counter a given answer, he must put on his shades as a signal that he disagrees and he has the hard cold facts to prove it. Often other students will come forward to either counter Student 2 in support of Student 1, or add additional evidence to support Student 2.

As a reminder, this type of discussion only works if you are holding steadfast to your NO TONE ZONE policy, which includes inappropriate body language. Otherwise, it will become more argumentative than productive.

Wait Time

When you're facilitating question and answer sessions with the whole group, wait at least five seconds before you call on a student to answer the question (Marzano, 2007, p. 108). It might look something like this:

I want you to THINK about this question for a moment. Why was it imperative the characters head for high ground when they heard the siren?

Then wait, scanning the class, counting in your head, 1, 2, 3, 4, 5. Little by little, the number of hands up in the air continues to grow until nearly, if not all, the class's hands are up.

This simple technique will stop you getting answers from the students who just throw their hands up in the air even if they haven't completely thought out the answer. It will also allow the students who process more slowly to pull out the information, think about it, and formulate their answers. Don't mistake slow processing for poor thinking. On the contrary, these students are often extremely bright and frequently come up with interesting answers—if you give them the chance. However, if you only call on the students who can quickly recall information, the slower ones will eventually stop attempting to recall the information altogether—and they will stop learning. Of course, you'll never know how bright they are if you don't give them opportunity to search their data banks for the information.

Many of the students our education system labels as *slow* or *underachieving* fall into this category. Be the teacher who allows them to realize their potential, simply by giving them time to think about their answer.

Classroom Snapshot

One of my students had a huge problem with processing. It took him longer to retrieve the information and longer to get it out. By the time he reached my class, most teachers had stopped ever asking him a question. If you did, he would stumble and stammer until everyone, including the teacher, got fidgety. The upshot was that he had stopped even starting the retrieving process. He figured after all these years, why should he even attempt to try.

For this student, being given the wait time was a blessing. It gave him the opportunity to retrieve, and then I would give him time to explain. Yes, in the beginning it was often painful to listen to him stumble over his words. But then, something miraculous happened! Almost overnight, he stopped stumbling over his explanations. It was as if, with a little practice and safe in the knowledge that he wouldn't be ridiculed, that part of his brain had switched on again.

Today, this student is achieving higher than anyone had imagined. His mother is astonished at his accomplishments in school. And everyone has noticed his new, positive attitude.

Turn Tos

Turn Tos will further support students who process slowly and help shy students who don't like talking in front of the class. When you ask a question, give the usual wait time for students to generate an answer in their head, and then ask them to turn to their neighbor and tell them the answer. This allows students to practice giving their answer to just one person before they have to repeat it in front of the whole class.

To keep them on track, walk around and monitor their conversations. This is less to make sure they are on topic, and more to make sure they are heading in the right direction. Then, to ensure that *both* students have been participating, when you reconvene as a group, periodically ask a student to explain their neighbor's answer. This is the key to accountability. Your students don't know who you will call on, and they know they have to be able to explain what their neighbor said.

Stop and Jots

After a few minutes of lecturing or reading a passage, **stop** and pose a question about the material and ask your students to **jot** down the information. They can jot on an index card, sticky note, or in their notes. Then they immediately share their information with a neighbor, pass it on to the next person at the table, or simply share it orally with the entire class. Whichever you choose, your students will be manipulating the material internally, making sense of it, sharing their ideas, and clarifying their thoughts.

I DO, We DO, They DO, Partner DO

When you introduce a new concept, you need to build up to partner work. Here's a useful process that gives your students many chances to manipulate information, with a slow release from the teacher's instruction, as well as a slow increase of independence.

I DO: Do a few problems yourself to allow your students to follow your explanations and procedures.

We DO: When they get a general sense of the process or idea, ask them to do a few of the problems with you.

They DO: After one or two problems, allow them try a few problems on their own. At this stage, walk around the room, checking over shoulders to see if they are on the right track. Stop and answer any questions they may have about a particular problem.

Partner DO: When most students have grasped the concept, break them into pairs and assign certain problems to practice. In a partnership, each person has a role: a coach and a player. Each partner is to complete the problem, but the player is in charge of explaining in step-by-step detail how they came up with the answer. The coach listens, questions, or compliments the player for a job well done. If the coach thinks the player is incorrect, she flags the error and shows the player an alternative approach on her mini-board. The two look at the problems, come to a consensus and, if there is a discrepancy, call the teacher over to adjudicate. At that point, roles are switched, and the student who was the player is now the coach and they continue practice. To ensure each student gets adequate practice on all styles of problems, include at least two of every kind of problem to solve.

This process stops one student from sitting back and letting the other person do the work, because each partner must take the reins and explain the process. Bear in mind, you have to explicitly teach your students this way of working until it becomes second nature. This means walking around, monitoring each partnership, complimenting those qualities required for good coaching—listening, good communication skills, rapport, inspiring and motivating comments—as well as making sure students are abiding by the rules, or some will take advantage and try to weasel out of the work.

At the end of their collaboration, make sure your students thank their partners for helping them practice the new concept. Give high fives or knuckle punches and offer each other a "Hey, good job today!" Applaud good work by both sides.

Classroom Snapshot

Using the *I Do, We Do, They Do, Partner Do* process has delivered tremendous benefits in my classroom. The biggest is improving my students' understanding of the work. I have found that by using this method, they understand the concepts quicker and deeper. I have to do far less reteaching, if any at all. In the end, the students learning from this method mastered the material and produced 100% on their assessments.

Use Deliberate Memory Strategies

Human beings need a trigger to retrieve a memory. You've probably experienced this yourself. Perhaps you promised a colleague to bring them something from home and you didn't remember until you saw them again the next day. "I'm so sorry, I forgot!" you say. But you didn't really forget—you just remembered at an inconvenient moment! We need to give our students convenient memory triggers that they can use during tests to recall the information they have learned.

Teach the Corners/Walls

Every room has corners and walls, making them ideal memory triggers (Jensen, 2008, p. 164). Here's an example of how you can use these triggers to embed memories. Suppose you're teaching the four basic types of sentences. Split your class into four groups and give each group a type of sentence. Challenge each group to create a sign and come up with a simple chant and gesture to teach all of us to remember the sentence types. For example, the interrogative sentence team might come up with:

Chant: "Things that make you go . . . hmmmm?"

Gesture: Put a finger on your chin and look up as if questioning something.

Hang the signs in the each corner and then, as a group, *learn each chant and gesture in each corner.* Standing under the appropriate sign, listen and watch a couple times, and then practice together as a class. Before you leave each corner, make sure you ask, "This corner will always be associated with what type of sentence?" And get the class to shout out the answer, "DECLARATIVE!" Then repeat it, "What type of sentence?" "DECLARATIVE!"

After learning each new corner, ask your students to repeat the other chants and, at the end, go back through them one more time for practice. For the next couple days, to start the class, visit the corners and sing the chants. While your students will know the chants on day one, this repetition over a few days will make sure they are stored in long-term memory.

You can use this technique to teach different properties of any type of information. It lends itself to distinguishing "mean, median, and mode," or similar, but different vocabulary, different geographic terms, or different historical events.

Classroom Snapshot

For years, I struggled to get my students to remember the four basic sentence types using the basic lecture/worksheet format. They'd remember for a moment, but the results of a review quiz a month later were always disheartening. Since learning this topic using the corners of the room, no one has ever failed a pop quiz.

Even a year later, when some former students were with me in a different room, out of the blue, one said, *Hey Mrs. Currie, I remember, that corner was declarative, that one was interrogative . . .* I had to know if anyone else remembered, so we all stood up and went to the corners, and every student remembered each corner and what distinction it held.

Body Pegging (using body location to remember)

Just as every room has corners and walls, so every student has a body, to which you can attach bits of information. Parts of the body are ideal memory triggers. For example, if you're teaching nonfiction text features, starting at the head, attach a feature to different parts of the body. So, for *captions*, place a CAP on your head. For *headings*, put your hands around your head and shake from side to side. Ask your students to help you come up with the gestures. They'll have fun and the memory will be even stronger. Middle schoolers love this type of activity—especially when they discover they can easily remember the information. Months later, every student will be able to remember the content via the location on their bodies.

Movement (using their bodies to remember)

Of the four memory pathways—reflexive, semantic, procedural, and episodic—procedural, our muscle memory, is the strongest, easiest to trigger, and longest lasting (Marzano, 2007, p. 54). Movement is also highly engaging—and fun! Whenever you can, make up movements to help your students remember.

For example, how can you get students to remember how to change mixed numbers into improper fractions? (Multiply the denominator to the whole number and then add that number by the numerator.) First, begin with your normal method of teaching. Do various problems showing the class the steps. Then ask your students to do a few with you. But then, bring in the big guns. Say to your students, "Now, in past years people found it hard to remember that they need to multiply then add the numbers, so I came up with a little jig."

Then demonstrate. Place your arms in front of you making an X, then simply turn them ever so slightly to create a + sign. Ask your students to stand up and teach them the multiply-and-add jig and song. Practice it together, practice with a partner. There'll be lots of laughter—this is good! Then, send them back to their seats and do a few problems together, using your arms to SHOW what to do, and get it into their bodies. Next, when students are working with their partners, keep circulating and ask individuals to show you the procedure (multiply and add) with their bodies.

When a student comes across a problem like this later, all you have to do is to ask them to raise their arms in front of them. This simple act will instantly trigger the multiply-and-add memory.

Classroom Snapshot

For many of my students, discovering that movement triggers actually work is a turning point in their learning. This is the first time they have ever found it easy to remember information. Of course, it does make testing time very amusing, with arms flinging here and there as the students use movements to recall how to do math problems.

Acting Out/Drama

Drama helps students to build an episodic memory pathway, which is the strongest and easiest memory to access. To dramatize a point, students must be fully engaged in the learning process. While preparing, they must first immerse themselves into the material to understand it. This requires them to read it, think about it, and create meaning and connections (Swartz, 2008, p. 27).

Drama also allows students to show what they know through a fun, yet highly memorable way. For many students, getting up and hamming it up in front of their peers is a strength not often capitalized on in the classroom. In fact, many teachers expend a lot of effort trying to squelch the drama in the classroom. Instead, why not leverage what kids already enjoy doing—dramatizing their point!

In Chapter 6, you'll find a sample lesson, called Reading Detectives, which relies on the heavy use of drama. There are countless other options. For example, you can dramatize vocabulary. Give each group a word and challenge them to create a skit that helps to define the word. In a few minutes, with improvised props, each group will have thought deeply about the meaning of their word. Then the class can sit down for a quick show and try to guess the dramatized words.

Or tell your students they have to make some models for the "wax museum." Here each twosome or trio are given a term the class needs to remember. Their job is to try to get the audience to guess what the term is. The catch is that they can't talk or move to define the word. They must position themselves in such a way that portrays the definition in a frozen or wax figure stance. They are permitted to use small props like a paper torch and crown in the case of identifying Lady Liberty in a particular scenario, but nothing else.

If you're pushed for time, try a thirty-second scenario activity. Here, students are given a word, for which they have thirty seconds to prepare a scene and thirty seconds to perform. Each student in the duo or trio must contribute to the scene in some capacity—whether acting, becoming a piece of background, or developing a prop, ensuring that everyone is working with the word, thus understanding and remembering its definition.

For all of the above activities, impress upon your students that the goal is not to stump their classmates, but make the definition so clear that everyone can recognize and remember it.

Every aspect of your curriculum offers opportunities for drama. Students can act out explorers discovering the new world, definitions of acute, obtuse, and scalene triangles, or a piece of food traveling through the digestive system. They can become sentences, molecules, figurative language, or points of a graph. The moment your students begin to act out your content, they are 100% engaged, guaranteeing stronger, longer memories.

Chants/Songs

Your students may not be able to remember your classroom content, but they know the words of all the songs and jingles. Put your content into a song and they will find it far easier to remember—especially if they made up the lyrics.

For example, to teach mean, median, mode, and range, first introduce the terms to your students, so they had a general idea of what these are and how to solve for them. Then divide the class into four groups. Give each group the starting two lines to the tune of "Row, Row, Row Your Boat." Challenge the groups to finish the last two lines by explaining how to solve for their term. So, they may sound like this:

Mean, Median, Mode, and Range
(Sung to "Row, Row, Row Your Boat")

MEAN

Line, line, line numbers

Neatly in a row,

Add and add and add and add

And divide by how much you know!

MEDIAN

Line, line, line numbers

Neatly in a row,

Least to greatest, cross them off

And that is how it goes!

MODE

Line, line, line numbers

Neatly in a row,

Select, select, select, select,

The one most often goes!

RANGE

Line, line, line numbers

Neatly in a row,

Shoot the high and shoot the low

Subtract and then you'll know!

If your students haven't had much exposure to writing their own lyrics, then make sure you give the first couple lines to start, as well as a simple familiar tune.

Murals

Ninety percent of the information that enters our brain is visual (Ritchhart & Perkins, 2008, p. 57). This is why we think in pictures. Every chance you get, encourage your students to tie word meanings to pictures.

One very popular way to do this is by creating giant murals. For example, after introducing your vocabulary words for the week, give each students a piece of chart paper to create a giant vocabulary mural. Using each of the words in some capacity, they must create a scene of their choice depicting the vocabulary definition through pictures or using some of the words through conversation within the mural. Through the conversations within the drawing, you'll plainly see if the student truly understands the meaning of the words. You want these murals to be detailed and thought provoking, so give your students several days to complete this assignment.

To take the giant murals one step further, the day they are due, conduct a class gallery walk. Here you post five murals at a time around the room. As a whole group, visit each mural. The owner of the masterpiece explains what they drew and how it defines the weekly words. The group may ask for clarification, definitions, or simply congratulate each artist and then move onto the next mural. Taking a gallery walk requires the owners to discuss and redefine their words after creating their masterpiece—offering another chance to embed the memory, as well as offering public speaking practice. It also acts as a review for the whole class.

Alternatively, create a backdrop mural. For example, if you're studying ancient civilizations, divide your students into tribes or civilizations to study and present. As one of their assignments, ask them to create a background mural depicting the scene/location/ housing representing their civilization. Give each group about six or seven feet of bulletin board paper to use. Students must fill the entire paper, which will then be hung behind them as a backdrop during their presentation. They are also required to describe what is taking place in the backdrop as part of their presentation.

Manipulatives

Students who are kinaesthetic thrive on active, hands-on activities. Manipulatives offer them an alternative memory aid. Try to design every lesson so students are touching something, moving something, or becoming something within the context of the lesson. Most worksheets can be re-created as a manipulative, simply by making them movable. For example, you might ask your students to cut out vocabulary word cards, match them to a card of synonyms, and glue them into a journal. Or, if students have to circle the correct form of the verb, then create the sentences on strips, and put all the answers on cards. As your students work through the strips, they must match the correct word by putting the card on the strip.

Classroom Snapshot

One year, I had three learning-support students who continually failed their spelling tests. So I designed a hands-on spelling activity for them, where they got the chance to learn how to spell words by manipulating little letter cards. As soon as I introduced this simple strategy, each of the students began acing their weekly spelling tests!

Key Points

- Collaborative learning helps students to process, understand, and recall information.
- When students collaborate, they come to appreciate the perspectives of and to work and communicate effectively with others—all critical social skills.
- Often, a student explanation creates the brightest spark of understanding with a peer.
- Competition is learned naturally, while cooperation must be *taught*—we need to teach our students collaborative skills.
- Make the physical environment conducive to collaboration.
- Create multiple opportunities for students to talk about new information.
- Use deliberate memory strategies to help students retrieve the information they file away.

4

Take a TEAMing Approach

Many—if not *most*—successful endeavors in life require people working together (Ritchhart & Perkins, 2008, p. 58). In a team, each person brings a unique set of skills, ideas, and input to the table. Then, working together, they create a result far beyond the reach of a single individual.

For example, building a house takes a large group of people, each with a specific skill set: architect, draftsman, bricklayer, plumber, electrician, and roofer. None of these individuals acting on their own can build the house. However, by working together and merging their talents, the team can achieve a significant outcome, often in a surprisingly short period of time.

Even endeavors that *appear* to be individual efforts are often actually the result of many people working together toward a common goal. For example, tennis players are often viewed as solitary athletes; however, the best ones always have a team of people behind the scenes contributing to their success—a coach, a physiotherapist, an agent, a financial advisor. Even someone who swims solo across the English Channel does not really swim alone. Beyond the camera, there is a team in a boat nearby, coaching, encouraging, and offering assistance.

Indeed, this book has two authors, but many other people have contributed to its final form, including our researcher, reviewers, editor, proofreader, and illustrator, whose contributions greatly enhanced the finished product you hold in your hands.

Learning in the classroom is very much the same. From the outside, it may appear to be a solo effort, but it's actually a team effort—and not just between student and teacher. Other students, administrators, parents, librarians, and occasionally tutors are all part of the learning team and can therefore help or hinder progress. As teachers, we cannot influence all of these stakeholders, but we can deliberately encourage other students to proactively support their peers while learning. And, we can play our role as coach—a vital part of the team.

In previous chapters, we've talked about the importance of engaging the whole class in creating an environment of trust and support, and of creating multiple opportunities for students to talk. This chapter takes these ideas one step further, by looking at how to create small (partnerships or groups), high-functioning learning **teams**—where students have the chance to learn more than they would working alone.

Why Does Working in Teams Enhance Learning?

As the previous chapter explains in detail, cooperative learning improves understanding and recall because talking about a topic requires the learner to process the information—the key to laying down long-term memories. Moreover, working in teams brings fresh perspectives to a learning situation and allows team members to help each other clarify concepts through discussion and questioning.

However, this is just the tip of the iceberg when it comes to the benefits of students learning in high-functioning teams. Teaming creates a supportive learning environment, which lowers blood pressure, improves immune systems, and increases attention. This is partly because a positive team environment provides a predictable transition between the students' world and the academic world, keeping stress levels low and eliminating threat responses. In addition, the sense of belonging that comes from being in a high-functioning team releases positive brain chemicals, such as serotonin, which make students feel calmer, happier, and more confident. This sense of confidence empowers students to have a go. With the safety net of their peers supporting them, this typically leads to small accomplishments—and a feeling of success—further empowering the student and continuing the virtuous circle. This momentum also has the side benefit of driving students to learn more, **without any extra effort by you, the teacher.**

Thus, team group work brings into play many of the brain-compatible teaching strategies, enhancing student learning and achievement. However, the above benefits are derived *only* from a high-functioning team. Merely putting students together, saying, "Hey you're a team!" and giving them a shared activity, rarely results in a high-functioning group. In fact, it typically leads to disaster. While this approach is possible with adults, this is only because they (hopefully) already have strong social and teaming skills. Few middle school students come with well-developed social, cooperative, or leadership skills. Most have difficulty saying, *Hello* to a classmate. If you throw socially inept individuals into a team environment, the team does not magically become a well-oiled machine.

Thus, to create learning teams, we must first explain to our students what that looks like and, second, teach them the skills to be a good team player.

What Does a High-Functioning Team Look Like?

Here are some basic ideas our students need to grasp about high-functioning learning teams:

- A team works together to achieve a common goal or shared purpose. This might be to complete an activity or simply to make sure that every team member understands a particular concept.

- All members brings with them complementary skills and individual life experiences that exceed those of any one person on the team.
- The team is aware of and draws on these different perspectives, strengths, skills, and knowledge bases.
- Teams encourage open discussion and actively solve problems together.
- Teams are mutually accountable. Meaning, members may be given individual roles, but these roles are still the responsibility of the team. This is why other team members will step in to help with a task, even if it is not their job.
- Teams are supportive of individual members' efforts— especially when they fail. Team members always feel safe to take risks in their learning.

The above points are important. Your students may sit at tables and occasionally work together on pieces of projects, but without conscious work, they will not develop the commitment, dedication, and cohesiveness of a team. Turning tables into table TEAMS takes time, patience, practice, and commitment from both teacher and students, but the end result is phenomenal—strong, dedicated, smart, achieving, brilliant young citizens—who eventually learn to work independently.

At the middle school age, students are desperate to gain their independence. They want the teacher to let go and allow them to discover much of the information on their own. They want to self-guide and self-check themselves and their partners. Yet, few are actually ready for this solo flight. Most need a safety net, because they usually crash on the first few tries. Working in teams or partnerships offers the illusion of independence, while providing a very strong safety net. It encourages students to try by themselves very soon after being introduced to new material—accelerating the learning process.

Creating a TEAMing Culture

In the context of this book, the four letters in the word *TEAM* all represent important qualities in building a TEAM culture.

Trust. As we discussed in Chapter 2, trust is the glue that binds relationships together. In a team environment, students must trust each other to be supportive at all times, especially if they try and fail. The teacher must trust the students to work independently. Students must trust the teacher to step in as coach and guide and to be scrupulously fair and always enthusiastic about any achievements—no matter how small.

Encouragement. All learners occasionally reach a point of wondering if they can actually do it—*can they really master this concept?* The on-going, ever-present encouragement of both the teacher and their peers is paramount to keep students moving forward, trying, testing, and exploring, until they climb higher and reach the next level of understanding.

Acceptance. The student's agreement to accept others, and be accepted by others, is often essential to eventual learning success. Feeling like an important part of a group naturally invites further appropriate risk-taking and exploration, leading to higher levels of success. In addition, knowing in advance one is fully accepted, regardless of the outcome of any effort, provides a safety net that keeps the focus where it needs to be—on the learning itself, not on what people will think.

Motivation. This is the driving force by which all of us eventually achieve our goals. *Extrinsic* (external) motivation often rises naturally in any group setting, as students encourage each other to succeed and rally together to achieve a common goal. *Intrinsic* (internal) motivation comes from an individual's personal interest in or enjoyment of a specific task. In teams, both interest and enjoyment are often increased when students are given the chance to share ideas and work together.

Notice that the common, underlying characteristic of these four themes is *emotion.* As previously stated:

Learning is always an emotional experience.

As teachers, the better we can actively construct a learning environment that protects and nurtures the emotional side of the learning process, the better the results will be. The careful and conscious cultivation of these characteristics vastly improves the chances of success for all students—in both large and small groups.

As a final incentive for teachers to put in the effort to establish high-functioning teams, please know that it's much easier to sustain the emotional health of a small team than a large group. In any large group of students, the challenge of keeping these characteristics operating at an effectively high level is quite demanding. Given the magnitude of the task, even the most compassionate and concerned teacher will occasionally miss something. Whenever our students work in teams, this pressure is reduced. While in teams, students take on much of the responsibility for remaining positive—temporarily removing most of this burden from the teacher. This means we do not have to remain at a high level of vigilance throughout the entire day—a virtually impossible task. Instead, for the times we do need to pay attention to every student, our focus will be *even better*.

The value of students learning how to work effectively in a team cannot be overstated. The positive outcomes that emerge from this opportunity ripple out in a variety of directions, and quite possibly influence students both academically and personally, for many years.

> *My teacher brings out the best in people. Well, at least me. She definitely makes me feel like I could try anything. She teaches us manners that will follow us forever.*
>
> —Brooke G.

Middle school offers ideal opportunities to give our students the chance, not only to learn *how* to work together successfully in small teams, but to *practice* these skills repeatedly, every day. This chapter shows you how to set up teams in your classroom and teach your students the skills they need to work effectively in a high-functioning team.

How to Take a TEAMing Approach

In a teaming classroom, students rarely work alone and the learning format is always changing. Try to build in equal opportunities throughout the day for whole group, table team, and partner pair work. Yet, as you swap between these formats, make sure the TEAM culture remains the same. Meaning, you need *Trust, Encouragement, Acceptance,* and *Motivation* present, no matter how big the group. There is no point honing interteam support but then allowing students to snicker when a classmate gives an incorrect answer in a whole group setting. As teachers, our priority is to foster a positive environment for learning before we introduce new content. This is the equivalent of tilling the soil. Our seeds of wisdom will not grow if students are tense, stressed, or feel unsupported.

So, the TEAM culture remains the same, but managing partner pairs or teams requires different skills. Therefore, this chapter is split into the following sections:

1. When to Split Up Into Smaller Groups

2. How to Set Up and Manage Partner Pairs

3. How to Set Up and Manage Teams

4. How to Coach From the Sidelines

When to Split Up Into Smaller Groups

Typically, we need to introduce new topics briefly to the whole group, before splitting into table teams or partner pairs, as appropriate. Partner pairs are ideal if the concept needs deep discussion and time to work through and develop understanding. If the content is relatively easy to grasp, but its details or terms are hard to remember, move quickly to table teams, so students can come up with memory strategies (see Chapter 5). In this case, it's vital that students learn the vocabulary or structure of a new concept, before they start discussing it. The following chart offers more ideas about the types of activities that suit different formats.

Whole Group	Table Teams	Partner Pairs
Introduce a lesson	Brainstorm	Brainstorm
Watch a video	Develop memory strategies	Discuss a concept
Interactive whiteboards	Practice new Information	Practice new information
Brainstorm	Preview/review lessons	Preview/review lessons
Read aloud	Correct HW or MW	Correct HW or MW
Meet-in-the-Middle	Projects	Center work
Review lessons	Games	Projects
Games	Carousel Walk	Timed reading/math tests
	Post-A-Point	Stop and Jots
		Chat and Check
		Think/Pair/Share

How to Set Up and Manage Partner Pairs

Mixing it up to work in partner pairs, not just table teams, is vitally important. Regularly working in partnership with different students over the course of a week helps students to get to know each other at a level that does not occur in a larger team. Thus, partner work helps to create the family atmosphere we are trying to achieve—where everyone knows each other's foibles, but is accepting because they are *family*. Moreover, the dialogue between two people usually goes deeper than the broader, but more superficial, discussions prompted by the different perceptions of a team with three, four, or five students. Finally, in a pair, both students have no option but to pull their weight.

Additional Ways to Establish Partner Pairs

In the previous chapter, we talked about creating apparently random pairs by drawing from Popsicle sticks or index cards printed with students' names on them. In fact, this is the easiest way to manipulate pairings if you need, for example, to avoid putting learning-support students together or to ensure a gender mix.

However, if you are happy with genuinely random pairings, you can introduce a brief burst of movement and fun by throwing your students into a quick game of "find your partner" using matching card pairs (mix together two decks of playing cards or super hero cards) or matching items. For some strange reason, small plastic fish are particularly popular with middle school grades. Alternatively, if you are short on time, you can simply say, "Turn to your neighbor."

Make sure students get different partners, rather than sticking with the same person all day. Your students want to mix and mingle as much as possible. Also, by changing partners frequently, you make sure no one gets stuck on their own with a person they don't particularly like for more than a few minutes.

To this end, you may also wish to introduce the concept of *appointment people* (see Appendix for a sample appointment sheet). This is the middle school equivalent of a dance card. The appointment sheet can be completed at the beginning of the year. Students go and ask other students to be their appointment person for this or that o'clock and write their names on their sheet—prearranging partners. Or, to make it more random, you can use your name cards and do the matching for them. Or, they can draw a name for each time slot. Then, you can call out, "Time for your 2 p.m. appointment." Students will check their sheet and rush to find their appointment person. Get your students to house their appointment sheets in their portfolio, which never leaves the room. Every few months, create new appointment person sheets, so students work with every classmate over the course of the year.

Working in a Player/Coach Partnership

To help your students have productive discussions when working in pairs, introduce them to the player/coach strategy. Tell them that to ensure both parties get time on the playing field, they must take it in turn to be a player (the problem solver) or a coach (the guide on the side). The player will be in charge of explaining their understanding and how they proceeded through the problem first. The coach is expected to listen intently, and guide the player through the problem if a need arises.

More specifically, when solving a problem, they must follow these steps before they swap over:

1. SILENTLY SOLVE—both team members silently solve the same problem.

2. CHAT and CHECK—the coach listens to the player's explanation, determining if she agrees or disagrees. If the player and coach agree, they move to the next step. If they disagree, the coach explains the steps she followed to come up with the answer. If the player disagrees with the coach's solution, the referee (teacher) is called in to assess and explain who is correct. Eventually, the pair reaches the correct answer.

3. PARTNER PRAISE—the coach says, "Nice job!"

At this point, the pair goes to the next problem, and switches roles.

When you first introduce this strategy, make sure you model both roles and clearly articulate what each person should be doing. For example, the coach should look at the player when he is giving his explanation, and *really* listen, because the coach will have to comment on what is being said. You also need to introduce appropriate vocabulary and a process for talking about the situation when there's a discrepancy between their answers.

For example, if the coach believes the player's answer is incorrect, rather than saying, "That's dumb!" you might suggest she kindly say, "I disagree with your answer." Then, she must back this up with hard cold facts, explaining in step-by-step detail, how she came upon the answer. This is also the moment to remind your students that this is a NO TONE ZONE, and telling your partner they are wrong is the worst possible moment to let a tone creep into your voice.

In the case of a disagreement, the player listens to the coach's rebuttal, to see if he made a mistake in his reasoning—quite frequently the reason for the discrepancy! However, if pairs cannot agree through this process, they can now raise their hands and tell the teacher, "We think we have a discrepancy." At this point, both students explain their work to the teacher, and together come to a final consensus. Sometimes they are BOTH wrong, and therefore need to go back to the drawing board. A great learning lesson!

Classroom Snapshot

Heads bowed low over the book, not a peep is heard between Brooke and Journey as they scribble something into their reading journals. Brooke looks up and over to Journey, *I'm almost...yep...I'm done! OK*, Brooke says, *I'm the player on this question. So here goes. I believe the reason Mr. Pike...* she finishes her explanation. As she does, Journey sits there, looking at her partner and listening intently. When Brooke is finished, Journey adds as the coach, *Good explanation Brooke. I do agree with you, but I also added...* Brooke responds, *Oh, that's a good addition. Give me a minute to add that to mine.* She jots down the additional information and they swap roles to start the next problem.

How to Set Up and Manage Table Teams

Here are the answers to some frequently asked questions about setting up teams in the classroom.

How do I make this work in a departmentalized classroom?

The following ideas are explained for a self-contained classroom. But they have also been tested in departmentalized teaching environments, where students keep their books and supplies in lockers and teachers can have up to seven different classes in one day. Here are the adaptations that make it work in this situation:

- Color-code team supplies so every period has its own supplies and its own color.
- Keep these supplies in draws or portable tubs labeled by class period.
- Where possible, designate an area or shelf solely for text books used during a particular class period so various students can use the text books.

How many students per team?

The best numbers for table teams are between three and five students, depending on the size of your class. Smaller groups ensure greater individual participation, contribution, and accountability to their team. If your teams are larger than five, it's too easy for individuals to sit back and sponge off the others.

How often should teams change over?

To keep your team dynamics fresh and friendly, try to establish new table teams every two weeks. This gives students plenty of time to get to know each other, but not enough to get tired of each other. Don't worry if you lose a few days to holidays or snow days. Change every two weeks anyway.

How do you establish team composition?

As the teacher, you choose who goes on which team. It's worth keeping a team roster, so you can track who's been with whom and when students were last put together. Try to have a mix of boys and girls at each table, and include at least one relatively organized student. Clearly, at the beginning of the year, you'll have to take a shot in the dark in terms of who might be organized. Also, limit the number of learning-support students (who are frequently pulled out) in each team. Don't worry about putting friends or enemies together. In the middle school years, friendships and fallings-out come and go as fast as the wind, so there's no point trying to take them into account. In particular, resist the temptation go to the grade level below to ask opinions on who might get along. In your classroom, *everyone* has to get along. As already discussed, you are not asking students to marry each other, just work collaboratively for a small length of time. Remember, they will not be working in their teams all the time. There will be frequent breaks for whole group work and partner work.

When you first discuss team composition, it's useful to point out that the ability to work with different individuals is an important life skill—part of growing up and vital to success in the workplace. You might refer to yourself and say, "There are people on our staff that I don't care for. Have you noticed?" Wait for some head shakes. "Well, that's because I know I have to work with them, so I do, and I get the job done."

How do students know where to sit?

At the beginning of the year, identify where individual students sit, using their individually named survival bag. Students then stay at this table for two weeks, but are required to rotate seats every day, generally at their discretion, to get a fresh perspective of the room. On team turn-around day, use your named Popsicle sticks or index cards to identify student positions at their new tables.

What if I don't have tables?

If you have a room like a science lab that doesn't allow for round tables, you can still easily create teams by dividing the room into sections. Then you can simply identify each section as a different team. Tables don't make the team; they are merely a location device. It's the bonds, trust, and camaraderie that matter most in creating teams.

Do teams need their own supplies?

Yes! This helps their sense of belonging and greatly adds to the levels of organization in your classroom. So label your tables 1, 2, 3, 4, or A, B, C, D and create matching labeled storage tubs for table supplies. Thus, Table 1 has a matching Table Tub 1. Store your table tubs in a central location. Team leaders, or students chosen by their leader, are expected to grab the tub on their way in, and put it back on their way out of my class. During classroom hours, table tubs are always set in the middle of the table for every student to access at a moment's notice. Your table tub supplies might include

- Pad of sticky notes
- Index cards
- Stickers (little dot ones)
- Set of markers
- Two sets of colored pencils
- Scissors (enough for the entire table)
- Calculators (enough for the entire table)
- Rulers (enough for the entire table)
- Glue sticks (enough for entire table)
- Absent Folder* (Pocket folder)

*If a student is absent, his team is responsible for collecting the work and placing it in the absent folder housed in the table tub. That way, when the student returns, all his paperwork is already pulled together, not by the teacher, but by his tablemates.

At the beginning of the year, ask your students to label all the supplies going into the table tub. This makes it easy to reallocate the supplies at the end of each day. With students going off to do partner pair work, supplies will travel the length and breadth of your classroom. If you don't label individual supplies, there will be disputes about which supplies go where. If you have more than one class, you can set up the same system with different colors for each class.

Put a list of supplies on the tubs lids and make each team responsible for keeping their supplies neat and replenished. So, if a marker runs out of ink, students must turn it in to you before receiving a new one. At the end of the two weeks, check each tub to make sure it has all the appropriate supplies. If supplies are missing, students on that team either need to locate them, or replace them from personal items, or pay a *fine*—perhaps a "brain buck" per missing item (see Chapter 5).

Every once in a while, the Table Tub Fairy might visit your classroom during the night. She is on the lookout for clean, organized table tubs. If she finds particular tubs clean, she leaves behind a coupon for a free trip to the treat jar/prize box.

Where do we store textbooks?

Give each team a designated, labeled bookshelf for storing all team textbooks. So, if a student starts the week at Table 1, then she will store her books at Shelf 1 for the next two weeks. Teams can decide how to organize the books on the first day of team turn-around. For example, they may choose to sort by subject (all social studies books together) or by student (each team member's books together).

Make your teams responsible for organizing and gathering the material they will need each day. Teach your students efficient ways to do this. For example, rather than the entire class charging up to the shelves and gathering their own books, the team leader should delegate one person from each team to gather all the textbooks needed for their table. If multiple supplies are needed, like chart paper or mini-boards, various teammates will be asked to gather the different materials. Once your teams are organized, you can expect this whole process to get done in twenty to thirty seconds. To save time in the morning, write all the supplies teams will need on your board. Then early students can start to gather them.

Changing Over Team Textbooks

Because your teams change every two weeks, students' textbooks must change location as well. This may sound inefficient, but if students kept their books at a particular book shelf all year, a team materials manager may have to scour four or five different bookshelves look for a team member's books. This takes too much work and too much *time*. With team textbooks already on the team shelf, the materials managers go straight to their designated shelf, grab the books, and off they go!

Therefore, on team turn-around day, you need a **ritual** to get new members books to the correct designated shelf. Here it is:

1. Old teams gather back together, and count off, 1, 2, 3, 4.

2. When the music begins, Team 1 runs off and gathers one type of book, let's say, spelling. They come back, give Team 2 a high five, signaling Team 2 to gather the next set of books. Team 2 comes back and high fives Team 3, and the process continues until all the texts are collected.

3. While students are waiting for the gatherers, they begin to organize the books into individual piles.

4. Once the books are separated, each student takes his or her own books back to the new team table. The process begins all over again, except in reverse, with each student taking a different type of book and placing it on their new shelf.

By midyear, if not sooner, your classes will come right in and start organizing their books without you having to ask.

Where do students store their own supplies?

Provide, or ask your students to bring in, individual pouches to hang on the back of their chair, to store individual notebooks, pencil cases, and portfolios. These pouches allow for quick access to frequently used materials and can be easily moved when students switch tables every two weeks.

Classroom Snapshot

Over time, my teams transform into well-oiled machines. No more do they need the leader to tell them what to gather. When they enter the room and read the whiteboard, you will often hear individuals say to their teams, *I'll get the whiteboards!* and another say, *I'll get the workbooks!* Not only that, but if the entire class needs their minioffices, which are all housed in a central location, one person usually takes it upon themselves to hand them out to the entire class.

Setting Team Expectations

Before you can establish teams, you need to establish a general classroom understanding of what it means to be in a team—or they simply will not work! Early on, lead a class meeting to discuss that you will be working in teams this year, covering the following points:

- Teams are temporary—it's only for two weeks.
- Team members must bond, by coming up with a team name, cheer, rubric, and mascot.
- Team members will have many chances to work outside of their team daily—so don't stress if you're not thrilled with all your team members.
- Teams MUST remain teams for the duration—no exceptions.
- Team members must understand HOW to collaborate—the NO TONE ZONE has never been more important.
- All team members will be held accountable for equal workloads.
- Teams are ALWAYS collaborative, NEVER ever competitive.

Getting Student Buy In

Students who have never been in a team environment, or have been involved in poorly-managed teams, may balk at the news that they will be working in teams. A common concern is the belief that they will be stuck in the team forever with people they don't like, or that they will get stuck doing all the work while others sit back. The above discussion will help to alleviate many such concerns, but is unlikely to produce any real enthusiasm for teaming as a concept. This is why the initial team synergy assignment *Building a TEAM Tower* (see Chapter 2) at the beginning of the year—or whenever you first introduce teaming—is so important.

As a reminder, this activity sees each team trying to build the tallest tower using straws and masking tape. Critically, the activity is debriefed to draw out the characteristics that make teams successful. This leads to Part 2 of the activity, where teams develop their own rubric and become largely self-governing. This activity is also very important because it builds student understanding of how powerful teaming is—they experience good and bad teaming firsthand and see the very different results between teams that work well together and teams that do not.

Here's a follow-up activity to cement the idea that working together leads to success. It uses a Glowing Energy Ball[1] to dramatically demonstrate the importance of everyone participating. This small plastic ball has metal strips connected to a tiny lightbulb. When you touch the strips simultaneously, the ball lights up and

---

[1]You can buy one for $3.50 from http://www.arborsci.com/energy-ball

hums. To demonstrate the power of participation, ask your students to stand in a circle. Hold the ball up and ask your students what they have learned so far about teamwork. Next, to drive home the point about participation, tell your class that *together*, you can light up this ball. However, if even one person doesn't participate, the ball won't work. Ask your students to touch fingers to connect the circle. The two students nearest the ball each put a finger on one of the strips. As soon as the circuit is complete, the ball will light up. Now ask just one pair to lose finger contact. The light immediately goes out.

Debrief the activity by saying,

*So, you see, if there is a break in the chain, the
ball will not light up. Just like in life, if there is a break in a
working relationship, the current will be weak or nonexistent.
Therefore, together we can make each other's light glow by holding on.
But if we let go, even for a moment, we allow someone's light go out.
And of course, we want everyone in the room to be glowing stars.*

Building Team Bonds

Whenever you form new teams, it is well worth spending time for each team to develop a team name, cheer, rubric, mascot, or logo. The first time your class forms teams, this process yields excellent coaching opportunities, where you can model appropriate team behaviors before your teams start working on content. Even when your students are adept team players, this bonding time remains important. It both helps to promote a sense of identity for the new group and allows team members to practice cooperating with students they may not know very well and get used to each other's idiosyncrasies and rhythms.

Team Names

Each team brainstorms to generate a team name. Names could be based on things students have in common, generated by get-to-know-you games. Or, you could set a theme, such as favorite colors, seasons, music, or holidays. Where appropriate, you could base the theme on a unit of study. For example, if you're studying ancient history, your teams could be the Aztecs, Maya, Anasazi, or Inca—and you could assign research projects appropriately. Or, during the Olympics, each team could choose a country, whose medal tally they could then monitor.

Team Rubrics

To hold students accountable, they should also create and fill out a behavior/collaboration rubric.

Team Rubric 1

TEAM NAME: _____

	M	*T*	*W*	*R*	*F*	*M*	*T*	*W*	*Th*	*F*
Homework Complete										
Group Cooperation										
Group Participation										
Team Spirit										
Team Organization										
Having FUN!!										
Learning New Information										
Here on TIME										
Daily Jobs Complete										

TEAMS: You will have 7 minutes to create this rubric on a large piece of chart paper.

Work together, make it colorful and NEAT.

Rating system: Always—5
                      Sometimes—3
                      Rarely—1

Team Rubric 2

	M	*T*	*W*	*R*	*F*	*M*	*T*	*W*	*R*	*F*
Leader kept team organized										
Team paid attention										
Team asked good questions										
Team developed conversations										

(Continued)

(Continued)

	M	T	W	R	F	M	T	W	R	F
Teammates were supportive to one another										
Team used best manners										
Assignment books are filled in and checked										
Daily Jobs complete										
Today I learned... Name 1										
Name 2										
Name 3										

TEAMS: You will have 7 minutes to create this rubric on a large piece of chart paper. Work together, make it colorful and NEAT.

Choose a system of rating your team. Example: 1–10, 1–5, a certain amount of stars, smiley faces, checkmarks, or think of your own rating system.

It's useful to design these on giant chart paper, large enough for all members to participate in the act of creation. At the end of every day, team members pull out their rubrics and collaboratively score themselves based on their time together. This is a good moment for you to walk around and monitor progress, making sure all members are putting in their opinions. Lean in and listen, and give positive reflections to the groups, *Yes, I agree, this team was VERY cooperative today, you deserve a 10! Oh, team, how come you only gave yourselves a 5 for cooperation?*

Team Cheers

Team cheers help to bring energy and positive emotions to your table teams. It's impossible to join in without smiling and laughing and getting caught up in the energy of your teammates. Ask each team to come up with a crazy, energetic cheer based on their name, with matching gestures or routines, for example:

- Myapan, Myapan, we bring war (Ancient Indian projects).
- Arms, arms, we put them in the middle when we do our cheer. Arms, arms, gooooo arms!!

- Go Green Bay, all the way (Super Bowl week).
- Mulberry Street, Mulberry Street, I saw it on Mulberry Street (Dr. Seuss Week).
- I throw my Skittles in the air some time saying A O—Taste the rainbow (candy theme).

This is not just about bonding. You can also use team cheers as a management tool. Students can use them to alert you when their team has completed an activity and is ready to be checked. You can also set it up that, when you want students to line up or come to the meeting area, a team cheer is the signal that all team members are organized and ready. This gives teams an incentive to get ready—each wants to be first to give their cheer—and provides a series of hurry-ups for those lagging behind.

Team Mascot/Flag/Emblem

These are optional. If you have time, ask each team to draw a mascot, flag, or emblem to create a colorful team placemat for their table. This will include the team name and cheer.

Encouraging Team Functionality

Team Leaders

Each table team has a daily team leader. On Day 1, this student is selected via an arbitrary process. For example, the new leader will be the team member who

- Has a birthday closest to today
- Is sitting closest to the windows
- Lives furthest away
- Is wearing the most red
- Has the smallest feet

The next day, the previous day's leader chooses his successor. Each team leader is in charge of keeping his team organized and pumped up. Responsibilities include

- Assigning go-getters
- Signing assignment books
- Encouraging her team to ask good questions
- Making sure teammates know where they're supposed to be
- Filling in the team rubric score

- Leading cheers
- Praising team efforts

Changing the leader every day gives every student—especially those who would typically sit back and do nothing—the opportunity to lead a team. Setting up team leaders can also save you, the teacher, a lot of work. You can ask team leaders to check assignment books, or make sure everyone has his homework in his bag ready to go home. Team leaders will make sure everyone is on the same page or that all the papers are named or in alphabetical order.

To get students to step up, for the first six weeks especially, make a big deal of students currently occupying the leadership role. You want your class to think that being a team leader is VERY important! Make sure you constantly check in with your team leaders. Compliment them constantly and give them high fives. Be very specific with your compliments; for example, you might say

Oh, I notice this leader has his team organized. I know that because all his teammates are on page ___.

I just heard this team leader compliment a teammate on a job well done! That shows me this team works well together!

This team leader just said Please and Thank You!

Through comments like these, everyone will pick up on what you expect from well-running teams. Every time you make a comment, leaders who aren't as organized or supportive will make a huge effort to get their act together.

As the year progresses, you may find that teams often begin to work naturally together, with everyone sharing the workload. Often, they decide they don't need a specific daily leader for major things, just for incidentals such as assigning teammates to gather material. This is fine, as long as your teams are functioning well. Frequently, around Christmas, students seem to forget how to monitor their behavior. At this point, you may need to reinstate your intense support of team leaders and go back to complimenting them all the time, until they pick up their game.

Keeping Teams Tight

Every week, throughout the year, use a simple five to ten minute activity to keep your teams tight. Once your students adapt to teaming, it's tempting to save time by leaving these activities out. In fact, five minutes of team building will actually save you time, because it keeps team synergies alive. It's often helpful to designate a day of the week for team building. Then your students will remind you if you forget, because they look forward to seeing what you have planned for them.

You'll find vast quantities of team building games on the internet, as well as books. A good place to start is Tom Heck's (2009) book, *Duct Tape Teambuilding Games—50 Fun Activities to Help Your Team Stick Together*, published by Life Coach, Inc.

Take the time to find activities that you are comfortable with and work for your students. In the first few months, try to steer clear of team building games that require hand holding or any type of touching until your students feel comfortable with each other. Otherwise, they'll spend the whole time worrying about cooties.

Here are a few tried and trusted suggestions to get you started:

- **7/11**—standing in a circle, students start counting clockwise, with each student saying the next number. But whenever the counting reaches a multiple of 7 or 11, that student only nods her head, and the counting path is reversed. If someone gets it wrong, the team has to start again.
- **Knotted Hands**—small groups stand facing each other, reach out, cross their hands, and grab another hand. They should be in a BIG knot. When the music plays, they must unknot themselves without letting go.
- **Tie Those Shoes**—small groups stand in a circle, untie, take off their shoes, and place them in the center of their circle. Now, while holding hands, each member must put their shoes back on and tie them without letting go! (Hint: holding pinky fingers is the easiest solution!)
- **Tower of Cards**—each group gets a deck of playing cards, and five inches of masking tape. Their goal is to build the tallest tower with only the given material in an allotted amount of time. Kick it up a notch and only allow students to use one hand!
- **Lean on Me**—starting in partners, sitting on the floor back-to-back, twosomes interlace their elbows, and push against each other to stand. What's great about this game is that it takes BOTH partners effort and *push* to get them standing—this offers a great lead-in to reminders about working together. From partners, you can move to small groups, and finally the whole class joins elbows and pulls each other up!

Ensuring Individual Accountability

Many teachers are put off using teams for fear that certain students will sit back and let the rest of the group do the work. To avoid this, make sure your team leaders number off to assign questions. It might sound like, "Leaders, number off your table." Leaders, pointing and counting off their tablemates, "Lindsey, you're 1, Aaron, you're 2, Tanner, you're 3, and Jacob, you're 4." Each person is then expected to complete the assigned problem and be ready to explain how it was solved.

If a table is working together on various problems, ALL members are expected to be able to know the procedures to the solution. They need to understand that, at any given moment, any member of the team may be called upon. If a student is not clear on the reasoning behind an answer when called upon, either let her call S.O.S. or ask her to conference with her team and try again in a few minutes, when you get back to her. Make sure you call on students at random, sometimes asking more than one person on the team.

Ending Team Clean Routine

This is a life saver for the teacher, leaving the classroom sparkling clean and organized, with everyone leaving in a positive state of mind. It also helps all students to remember their homework. Teaching it in the first few days also yields excellent opportunities to model good teaming behavior.

Here's how it works. When the ending song plays, that signals teams to chant—1, 2, and 3, Let's GO! This is the signal for the following activities:

1. The team fills out the team rubric.

2. Team members gather what they need to take home.

3. Students chant 1, 2, 3, CHECK US! The teacher quickly runs through the list of material needed for the night, and the students double-check they have everything. If not, the teacher leaves so the team can reorganize and call again when they think they're ready.

4. If done, the teacher and students chant together, 1, 2, 3, LOCKERS! and the students go to their lockers and gather their coats and anything else that's going home.

5. Students complete their daily team jobs assigned by the team leader—packing away supplies, washing the tables, or picking up from the floor.

6. When their jobs are done, the students chant, *1, 2, 3, CHECK US!* The teacher checks through the list of jobs to make sure they are complete. If not, the teacher leaves again until she is called back.

7. If done, teacher and students chant together, *1, 2, 3, SEE YA!* The team lines up at the door.

Other than checking the teams, your job during this process is to encourage team members to help their teammates complete their jobs. Team leaders don't officially have an end-of-the-day job, but they soon learn that helping each other gets them out the door much faster. You might encourage others to step up as well, saying things like, "Whose job is it to sweep? Do you think someone can help Jessica sweep? It looks like she is still filling her book bag."

Classroom Snapshot

Team Turn-Around Day

Before school, I look in my team binder to see who was in which team in the past two weeks. As I decide where everyone will go, I place name cards in the middle of each table, so students immediately know what team they are now on, and which table is theirs. I also jot down the names in my team binder so I have future reference of who teamed up with whom.

(Continued)

(Continued)

On the whiteboard, a message appears:

Today is TEAM Turn-Around Day! Find your new table, switch your books, and create a TEAM name, cheer, rubric, and logo.

On the back table, I lay copies of TEAM rubrics and chart paper. Now I wait . . .

Five minutes later, the bell rings and students begin to enter the room, read the whiteboard, look for their names on the tables, and start executing the Team Turn-Around. Jason smiles, *Hey, Brooke, we're on a team together this week!* She responds with a smile, *Oh, cool! I already have an idea for a name!*

On the other side of the room, Haley has found her card on Table 3. She quickly locates her books from Shelf 2, the group she was in last week, and swiftly moves them to Shelf 3. As she is doing that, she also notices that Courtney will also be using Shelf 3, so she moves her things as well.

At Table 1, Isaac has grabbed a rubric and chart paper. Since all his team members have moved their books, they begin to create the rubric together. All hands are on deck—everyone is participating in constructing the rubric.

Nearby, at Table 2, four students ponder over a team name. *How about the Jazzy Jack-o-Lanterns?* Hope suggests. *No, let's create something that has to do with panthers, since it's spirit week,* someone else proposes. With that, they agree on a final name, and develop a logo.

Up front, members from Table 4 are checking in their homework. They worked well together this morning and have all their books moved and organized, their rubric is made, they have a team name, logo, and cheer. They are eager to share!

By 8:20, the morning song begins to play as teams finalize their cheers and double check to make sure they have all their belongings switched and organized. Time remains, so the teams can share their new names and cheers!

How to Coach From the Sidelines

When your students are in teams, it's tempting to retire to your desk. In fact, you have a very active role to play. Your students will be happy working in teams, but only if they know you will be there whenever they need assistance. So you always need to be visible and audible, offering coaching and guiding advice. You never give up the reins entirely, but neither do you lead from the front. Instead, like a good athletics coach, you are a guide on the side, always modeling, monitoring, and acting as an arbitrator, and giving constructive feedback or encouragement—as required.

When monitoring, as you walk around, if a pair is struggling, you can hover over these individuals a bit more to make sure they're getting it. If you have mixed ability pairs, make sure you monitor to make sure both students are doing equal shares of work. All the time, build on all the positive work you see by announcing it to the class.

When giving constructive feedback, be aware that this is a key ingredient for accelerating learning. Catching misunderstandings and making clarifications immediately increase the speed of understanding, and virtually eliminate the need to reteach something your students have learned incorrectly (Marzano, Pickering, & Pollock, 2001, p. 96). Additionally, catching students doing something correctly gives them confidence and increases their drive to want to do more. Also, providing feedback allows you to be extremely effective, because you can push able students further and further.

Sometimes, there are moments when you need to step in as a coach and intervene. For example, perhaps some team members are slow and continually holding the others up. The more organized team members are getting impatient. This is where you step in:

Teacher: "What do you see as the problem here?"

Students: "John is too slow and is holding us back."

Teacher: "What is it that YOU can do as a team member to help John become better organized instead of getting angry at him?"

Students: "Well . . . I guess we could help him out by getting a book for him as he gathers his binder."

Teacher: "Yes, exactly. You need to help John learn to become better organized by showing him how you organize yourself. Some people are better at that than others. Helping is much more productive than getting angry."

Being a guide from the side is a highly rewarding role. As you mingle with your students, you experience learning in its raw state. You hear your students' thoughts, you see them learning to collaborate, and you experience their fears and frustrations. You come across important opportunities to correct misunderstandings, and to bond and build relationships with your students. You sit beside the student who is struggling, hurting and frustrated—and you make a **difference** by telling him, *I BELIEVE in you. I'm right here to help. I'm not going to let you fail*. And, most importantly, you witness and celebrate those magical *Aha!* moments. You see students as they hit the mark. Their eyes light up and they turn to you and say, "OH, I *get it* now!" This is the moment for you to give them a high five, and a great big smile— the moment you get to say, "YES! I *knew* you could do it!"

Classroom Snapshot

OK, final question, I bellow with my best game show host voice into a plastic microphone. *For the title of* BRILLIANT STUDENT of the DAY... *identify the adverb in sentence 10!* Hands are waving frantically all across the room.

OK, Jason... I haven't heard from you yet... what's the answer.

He reads, *The man ran quickly down the street. The adverb is* down.

I gasp and grab myself by the throat... *I can't... I can't... breathe... Oh, my gosh... I'm looking for the* <u>adverb</u> ... I begin to melt to the floor.

The class is screaming at Jason, *There's a better answer Jason! Save her, save her!* Jason looks again, WAIT! I KNOW it! I KNOW it! The adverb is QUICKLY!

YES!!! YES!!! YES!!!! I shout, springing up from my crumpled state. *That's right! The adverb is what everybody? QUICKLY!* the room roars.

I head straight to Jason and give him a knuckle punch and smile. *Brilliant save, I KNEW you could do it! Good job.* I step back to let Jason's teammates give him a round of high fives.

Key Points

- Teaming creates a supportive learning environment, which lowers blood pressure, improves immune systems, and increases attention.
- Middle school students lack the social, communication, and leadership skills to automatically fall into high-functioning teams.
- We must explain to our students how a team works and teach them the skills to be a good team player.
- We must provide equal opportunities for whole group, table team, and partner pair work.
- We must build a TEAM culture: T = Trust, E = Encouragement, A = Acceptance, M = Motivation.

5

Prime the Positive Environment

One of the fundamental stumbling blocks to teachers' implementing brain-based learning techniques is that many of the strategies suggested seem doomed to descend into chaos and anarchy. To a teacher already struggling to control a middle school classroom, the suggestion to let their students move around, talk, laugh, and have fun seems little short of madness. If a child can't sit still and work quietly, what will happen if you let them loose?

While understandable, from teachers who equate silence with learning, this line of argument misses the point. Every one of the above, apparently frivolous, suggestions has a purpose: *to enhance learning*. For example, moving keeps blood flowing to the brain and, properly guided, can help cement powerful kinesthetic memories. Talking allows students to process information, increasing their understanding and recall. Laughing helps students to relax and recharge. It reduces stress and increases energy, enabling students to stay focused and accomplish more. And, finally, if your students are having fun while they're learning, they will remain engaged for much longer, embed clear memories of the experience, and return to your classroom motivated and keen to learn more.

Any teacher employing these strategies mindfully will certainly have a noisier classroom than a colleague using lecture and worksheet. However, all evidence points to the fact that the quality of learning in a dynamic, high-energy environment will be far, far greater.

Of course, a teacher must still be able to maintain discipline in such an environment—to keep students on track, make them accountable, and ensure appropriate behavior. And, just as brain-based learning requires different teaching practices, it also requires different discipline tactics.

Traditional teachers typically have three main strategies for disciplining unruly students: shout, threaten, and punish. However, brain-based research tells us that none of these strategies is helpful in the learning context. When students are stressed, they secrete stress hormones, which adversely affect brain function—especially memory. During a perceived threat, our adrenal glands immediately release high levels of adrenalin. If the threat is severe, and even if the threat is low but persists after a couple of minutes, the adrenals then release the steroid hormone, cortisol. Once in the brain, cortisol remains there much longer than adrenalin; while it does, it can prevent the brain from laying down a new memory or from accessing already existing memories.

In his book, *Why Zebras Don't Get Ulcers,* acclaimed Stanford University neuroscientist Dr. Robert M. Sapolsky (2004) has shown that sustained stress can damage the hippocampus, the part of the limbic brain that is central to learning and memory. His research hypothesized that stress hormones divert blood glucose to exercising muscles. This serves to reduce the amount of glucose (or energy) that reaches the brain's hippocampus. The result is an energy crisis in the hippocampus that compromises our ability to create new memories.

In simple terms, this means that if we stress students by yelling at, humiliating, or punishing them, they stop learning and remain unable to learn for some time afterwards. Thus, brain-based teaching strategies make great efforts to avoid having to use such tactics, since they are clearly counterproductive to learning.

This is why U-Turn teachers approach discipline from the other direction. Rather than waiting for and then punishing bad behavior, U-Turn teachers constantly seek to *prime* the positive elements of the classroom experience. Once the pilot light is lit, they then continue to do everything in their power to keep the energy flowing in that direction. It is not just that threat situations are bad; positive emotions are . . . positively productive! So, rather than reacting to poor discipline with tactics that prevent learning, we should proactively support good discipline with three positive goals:

1. **Demonstrate**—students learn just as much from what teachers do as from what they say.

If the teacher is contemptuous of a student's response, the class will be too. Alternatively, if the teacher is accepting of difference, generous with her praise, and appreciative of every effort, this also rubs off on her students. We must remember that some students act out simply because they have never seen positive behavior modeled by the adults in their lives. We cannot expect students to behave appropriately if they don't know what that looks like.

2. **Facilitate**—one of the best ways to support our students in behaving appropriately is to make it easier for them to do so. This starts with our own expectations. If we expect a particular student to be a problem, our attitude toward them will be negative from the start. We will give them less leeway than other students, reserve our smiles for our *good* students, and generally treat the *bad* student with distrust and suspicion. This student will promptly pick up on our unconscious hostility,

react against it, and quickly fulfill our expectations of bad behavior—thereby justifying our attitude in the first place. This classic example of a self-fulfilling prophecy is reenacted in classrooms all over the world. If we expect a particular student to behave badly, they almost certainly will. Our expectations as a teacher are the greatest predictor of actual outcomes in our classrooms. Change our thinking, and we will change the outcomes.

We can also be proactive in making it easy for all students to behave well. For example, we can give clear instructions. You know that moment when you notice half the class has failed to open their books to the correct page? It's easy to get cross with those students and blame them for not paying attention. But let's look at what happened here. We were responsible for communicating that instruction. If half the class didn't understand it, perhaps we could have done a better job with our instructions. Instead of getting angry with our students, perhaps we should apologize to them!

Before you react to that suggestion with outrage—just think it through. What are we trying to achieve here? We want every student looking at the right page. How long will that take if we berate half the class for not paying attention? And how many of those students will be ready to learn when we've finished? Instead, what if we smile and say, "I'm sorry. I wasn't very clear about our page number. Please turn to page 27 and wiggle your pen in the air when you get there." Your entire class will be on the right page in seconds—and they will be smiling at you.

In many situations where teachers get frustrated with students, there are two sides to the situation. Is a student fidgeting because he is badly behaved, or because his teacher has left him sitting still for too long? Is a student doing the wrong thing because she deliberately chose to be obnoxious, or because her teacher didn't explain the activity clearly? Rather than blaming our students every time they fail to do what we want them to, we need to make a bigger effort to provide clarity around every single classroom activity. And we need to stop putting students into situations—such as sitting still and silent for too long—that are guaranteed to generate poor behavior.

Of course, there are times when students are simply behaving badly. But even in these circumstances, we should give them the benefit of the doubt. By taking the blame ourselves, we can often divert a student from going too far down the poor behavior route. For example, by saying in a genuinely concerned voice, "I'm so sorry, Hayley. I obviously didn't make that instruction clear. Let me try again," we are effectively offering Hayley a get-of-jail-free card. Of course, *we* know that the instruction was clear and Hayley is deliberately pushing the boundaries, but we also know that yelling at Hayley makes her dig her heels in still further. This simple tactic gets students back on track without shouting or making them feel stupid. The fact that they got away with acting out is irrelevant. We achieved our objective of guiding their behavior back in line. Moreover, they are likely to spend the rest of the lesson on their best behavior.

3. **Motivate**—it may seem counterintuitive, but many students misbehave because it's the only way they can get enough attention. For some middle school students, any attention is better than remaining anonymous—it proves they exist and affirms their sense of self. If these students can't get positive attention

by answering questions correctly or getting good marks, they will get negative attention by acting out.

This is why U-Turn teachers heap copious rewards on students for even minor improvements in behavior. These rewards can be anything from a private smile to public praise to a coveted prize. The key is to give these rewards constantly, frequently, and with great enthusiasm. If you used to spend fifteen minutes every day disciplining the same student, you need to spend at least that long praising his positive behavior.

In the U-Turn classroom, we proactively seek out the good in every learning moment. There is always something, somewhere that is praiseworthy in any well-intended learning effort by every student. This does not mean we should *invent* something positive. We need to start with the expectation that there's good in there somewhere—and do whatever it takes to find it. And, yes, this sometimes does involve some creative thinking!

The common analogy says that there are two types of people: those who choose to see the glass as half empty, and those who choose to see the glass as half full. Yet perhaps there is a third choice— a way to look at any situation from a completely different point of view. As comedian George Carlin once said:

> I just see a glass that's . . . twice as big as it needs to be.

This is the kind of thinking truly effective teachers need to fully embrace. To proactively encourage good behavior, frequently requires us to think about the world from a different perspective. This chapter offers specific strategies to help you do that. In the process, you will prime the positive environment and turn your classroom into a far happier and productive place for you and your students.

Classroom Snapshot

At first, I thought that some of these ideas were too "simple" and could not possibly make a difference. I could not have been more wrong. My "worst" year turned out to be the best one I have ever had. It all started with my attitude. I realized my students were living up to what I expected of them. When I did not believe in them, they underperformed.

> *Once I started to change the state of our classroom, the difference was immeasurable. Through hard work and a TON of social teaching, we reached 100% proficiency in science and math on the PSSA tests that year, and 98% proficiency in reading.*
>
> —Chris Straub, 4th grade teacher,
> Commodore Perry School District

How to Prime the Positive Environment

Demonstrate

Modeling is the number one way students learn, especially in terms of interpersonal communication skills. Therefore, if you want your students to interact positively with each other, then you must lead the way, by example, consistently demonstrating what you expect them to do. When you do this, here are three important principles to bear in mind:

1. Understand your attitude is contagious.

2. Be specific about the behavior you expect.

3. Find the itty-bitty bit of better behavior.

Understand Your Attitude Is Contagious

Be hyperaware that your class will mimic your reactions to individual students.

Every class has students who are different—those who move through life to the beat of their own drum or don't fit the mold. Often, they are too quiet, too loud, too heavy, or think too far outside the box. These are the students who are prime candidates to be picked on by their peers—leading to all kinds of class disruptions. They are also the ones most likely to get under your skin. Often, by the time the teacher witnesses the incident involving these students, the victims are retaliating against their persecutors and become the ones who get into trouble. It's easy to treat these students differently, especially if they disrupt lessons.

Instead, it's vital is to embrace their differences, and treat them exactly like all your other students. If you behave in this way, the rest of the class will too, reducing the number of incidents in your classroom.

Many of these students are not easy to like because of their divergent or abrasive personalities. You may actually have to tell your class, *that's who they are . . . and we will accept them and respect them for that special spark*. You may also have to work with your more challenging students to give them the skills to fit in. Once these students realize that you accept them and are encouraging the rest of the class to do so too, they will work on their attitude. Many of these students have yet to find acceptance at school. If they find it in your classroom, they will work hard for you.

Be Specific About the Behavior You Expect

Never go into a school year or semester assuming the students in your new class know how to be organized or well-behaved. Apart

---

Classroom Snapshot

I could tell Susan thought another student's suggestion was dumb, because it was slightly outside the box.

Her sour face said it all.

But I said, *That's BRILLIANT! Let's give your idea a try!*

Susan immediately smiled and got into the excitement. It was textbook mirroring.

from anything else, your expectations may be completely different from those of the teacher down the hall.

Start by showing and telling your students exactly what to do. For example, one of the first pieces of positive behavior to teach your class is when and how to say, "Thank you!" Students of middle school age need solid modeling to learn appropriate ways to interact with each other. Teach your students that, whenever they finish working with partners or groups of tablemates, it's essential to thank them. Explain that they benefited from the interaction/collaboration, so it's only right to thank them.

The first time you call an activity to a close, ask your students to turn to their partner/tablemates and thank them. First, model how it is done, making sure they look each other in the eye while they say those two very important words. When middle school students are first introduced to this form of courtesy, they tend to avoid eye contact and quickly leave the area. You need to discuss, as a group, how rude that is and how the other person might feel if you bolt away.

Classroom Snapshot

By the second semester, thanking a partner has become second nature and students do so without being prompted.

David (with a handshake): *Thanks for your help, Jason; I appreciated it!*

Once you've modeled the behavior and prompted it, the next step is to highlight desired behavior whenever you see it in action. This is one of the most productive ways to help your students find the right road to good behavior and learning—*telling them **what** they are doing **right***.

Try to be very specific in your comments, rather than just using broad compliments such as *nice job*. For example, you could say, "Hey, I notice John is organized. Look how nice and neatly his books are stacked and off to the side." Or, "I notice Courtnie is helping Carla find the correct page. That's what I call good teamwork."

When you do this, other students will often start to mirror the behavior, hoping to get noticed.

Find the Itty-Bitty Bit of Better Behavior

Once in a while, you'll come across that one student (or some years . . . an entire classroom) who just can't seem to do anything right. It seems as if she would prefer to do something bad to get your attention than something good. Often, this is because, for the last six or seven years, she has only received attention when she was being reprimanded. This is all she knows, so it is all she seeks. To change, that student needs to experience the feel-good chemicals that are released when she gets attention for doing something good. You need to literally retrain her brain to seek out good behavior rewards.

This requires finding a glimmer of good behavior in that student, which sometimes requires looking really, really hard. Good behavior for naughty children may be something so little you may not even consider it a good behavior. But if you start small, and they experience the wonderful moment of being praised, you can quickly build up to better and better behavior.

Facilitate

Just as we can model good behavior, we can also proactively set our students up to behave well. The following five strategies will help you to support good behavior in your classroom.

1. Expect goodness.

2. Give students the benefit of the doubt.

3. Make your directions clear.

4. Use engaging transitions.

5. Keep your students accountable.

Expect Goodness

No matter what other teachers tell you—or the size of the file that arrives with a particular student—begin the year by assuming that each child can achieve and will behave well. If you treat each student with respect and kindness, that is exactly what you will receive back. And if you expect good behavior, you are much more likely to get it. The worst thing you can do is buy in to the preconceived notions the school has built about your students.

Ignore the files. Find the goodness in every child, accentuate it with positive affirmations, and build on it. The results will be spectacular.

Classroom Snapshot

Year after year, I see students with major discipline problems turn into motivated, high-achievers. On one occasion, Rob arrived part way through the year, with a file an inch thick and a reputation a mile long. Instead of reading the file and listening to the gossip, I gave Rob a clean slate, treated him with respect and held high expectations for him. For a couple weeks, he sat in my room quite still, unmotivated and extremely angry. But as soon as he realized I really was on his side and believed in him, he relaxed. Gradually, he transformed into a team player who could control his anger and work productively with his group. His grades rose and he came to school with a smile.

Give Students the Benefit of the Doubt

When a student appears to have misbehaved, resist the urge to yell first and instead ask questions. You may find the student who has brought in cash for a book order, instead of the check you specifically asked for, has raided his own piggybank because his parents wouldn't give him the money. Or the boy who hasn't done his homework sat in the emergency room all night with his mother. Or the girl who did her homework in pen, not pencil as instructed, didn't have access to pencils at home.

Often, by patiently digging deeper into the situation and asking *why*, you'll find goodness—not the bad behavior you initially perceived.

Make Your Directions Clear

In a dynamic classroom, with lots of movement and collaborative activities, clear directions make the difference between chaos and constructive work. Clear directions depend on one simple but rarely understood idea—we must always give directions *one at a time*. This incredibly simple, yet highly effective strategy will transform your teaching experience. Here's why it's so important.

Normally, teachers give multiple instructions at the same time. For example: "OK everybody, we are going to use appointment person 2 o'clock today, and you are going to read your story, making sure to fill in the remaining information. If you get done with that before the time is up, continue writing your essay. OK, let's go!"

What happens next? Let's look at it in slow motion. As soon as we say, "We are going to use appointment person 2 o'clock today," your students will start digging into their folders to look up their 2 o'clock person, waving to their person, or rolling their eyes because it wasn't the person they had hoped for. Thus, they fail to hear all of the following instructions, leading to a resounding chorus of, "What do we do?" This is hugely frustrating for teachers, to the point where they are put off trying to engage students in partner activities, because it always descends into anarchy.

The answer is astonishingly simple. Give directions one at a time, and don't move onto the next direction until the first one has been completed. So, the above instructions would work like this:

"OK, everybody, we are going to use appointment person 2 o'clock today. Find that person, go!"

(Play music until all have found their partner. Pause the music.)

"When the music starts again, please read your story, making sure to fill in the remaining information. (Start the music.)

(When some pairs are finishing . . .)

"Those of you who've finished, please continue writing your essay."

You may feel that giving directions in this manner slows things down, but in fact it saves you time because your students know what they're supposed to be doing and you don't have to repeat yourself.

Use Engaging Transitions

A large number of discipline incidents occur during transitions from one activity to another, or when activities are interrupted by a phone call or a classroom visitor. Typically, if students are allowed to disengage from the classroom between activities, they tend to gossip with their neighbors or disappear into their own worlds. At best, they take ages to reengage with the next activity—requiring teachers to nag and repeat themselves. At worst, the vacuum creates the perfect environment for boisterous students to get into trouble.

The first rule of engaging transitions is to use music, as covered in Chapter 2.

Music helps to make transitions fast and effective. Your students will respond to its signal far faster than they will respond to the same instructions followed by silence. For example, if you want to move the class from small groups sitting at tables to the rug:

Teacher: Please stand up! When the music begins . . .When?

Students: When the music begins!

Teacher: Come up to the rug. (Play fast, upbeat music.)

The music focuses your students on the task and drives them to their destination. You won't have to shout or nag students to hurry up; they will move at the pace of the music.

Response chants are also extremely effective at keeping students engaged, because they require the students to respond, which takes their full attention. Like all rituals, these need to be taught and practiced at the beginning of the year, and then refreshed periodically.

It's important to insist on chants being done correctly: they need to be short, crisp, and for some, end in silence. Practice with your class until it functions like a well-oiled machine, and then enjoy your newfound ability to control your students with a single signal. Here are some useful signals and responses to teach younger students. For older grades—who you think might be *too cool* for this—get them to make up their own chants. Tell them, "This class needs a chant to move us quickly from here to there. Work with a partner—you have one minute to come up with a suggestion. We'll vote on the best and rotate them over the year. Go!" Don't forget, chants are part of the teen culture, heard on the sports field and in movies about military training. If they own it, they'll chant it.

Need	Signal	Response	Comments
An unscheduled interruption requires everyone to be quiet and listen.	Blink the lights off once and say: *Pause for a moment please.*	Students all turn to face you and say: *Pause*	This gives you their instant attention, without having to raise your voice.
Every student needs to be holding a pencil.	Raise your hand in the air and say: *Pencils up, up, up.*	Students raise their pencils into the air and hold them there.	This allows you to see who is ready. Only proceed when **everyone** has his pencil up and ready to begin.
Students indicate they have a rebuttal to an answer.	Students put on dark glasses and cross their arms.		You can immediately see who agrees with the answer given.
You need silence to answer the phone.	Clap out the tune of "A Shave and a Haircut"	Students say: *Shh, shh* instead of *two bits.* Repeat and become silent.	
You need their attention fast.	*1, 2, 3, eyes on me!*	*1, 2, eyes on YOU!* Silence	Immediately tell them the reason you need their attention.
	5, 4 . . .	*3, 2, 1* Silence	
You need silence before leaving the classroom.	*Facing forward lips are zipped!*	*Lips zipped, ready to rip!* March out of the room.	Never say: *I'll wait for you to get quiet before we leave the classroom.* You'll be waiting for a **long** time!

(Continued)

(Continued)

Need	Signal	Response	Comments
You want students to bring certain items to the next activity on the floor.	*Please stand up and push in your chair.* *You need 3 things.* Hold up 3 fingers. *How many?* *A reading book, file, and pencil.* "*1, 2, what do you do?*	Wait for everyone to comply. *Three!* A reading book, file, and pencil. *3, 4, hit the FLOOR!*	This chant will spring your students into action, gathering their materials. The transition from tables to floor should take no more than thirty seconds.
You want students to turn to a particular page.	*Turn to page 13.* *What page?*	*13!*	

You can also turn regular activities into fun, transitional rituals. For example, this transition, designed for Grades 5 and 6—which you can sing out in military fashion—helps make sure every student gets their test paper headed up and ready to go in a fast, fun manner.

Teacher	Students
"It's time to head your up!"	(Repeat)
"Make sure you have your name and date."	(Repeat and write)
"Spelling Test"	(Repeat and write)
"Unit 4"	(Repeat and write)
"Number from 1 to 10"	(Repeat and write)
"And do it again"	(Repeat)
"But 11 to 20"	(Repeat and write)
"Skipping spaces"	(Repeat)
"Nice and neat"	(Repeat)
"Sound off"	(1, 2)
"Sound off"	(3, 4)
"Hard work pays off!" (Pound fists on the tables twice)	
"Let's go!"	*Students star each other's papers to ensure everyone has added his or her name.*

This will get your students quickly focused on the next task. It also fires them up for a test.

If you don't need to number the papers, you could end the chant this way:

Teacher	Students
"I have my name do you have yours?"	(Repeat)
"Yes, I do; how 'bout you?"	(Repeat)
"You better look at my paper too!"	(Repeat)

Keep Them Accountable

How do you stop students from veering off task when they are working in teams and partnerships? First, they need to know that, at any given moment, they can be called on to explain what they are doing or what steps they took to get to the point they are at currently. Second, you can use several strategies to keep them accountable:

- **Lean in and Listen**—when groups or partners are working together, roam around the room, stopping at each group to listen to their conversations. You can literally lean into their circle or grab a chair to sit for a moment. You'll quickly discover whether they are on task, if they comprehend the objective, if they know where they are heading next, or what meaning they are constructing from the activity. Leaning in allows you to reteach when necessary, commend fantastic ideas, and bond with students in a way that a large group setting just wouldn't make possible. Additionally, if a district requires anecdotal records on students, this provides the perfect opportunity to gather that information. Sometimes, when you hear commendable conversations, stop the whole class and explain what you just heard, or let the group share with the class what they found.
- **Drive-by**—this is similar to the lean-in-and-listen tactic, but faster. It's useful when you don't necessarily need to lean in and listen to conversations, but you still need to make sure students are focused and on task. For example, use a drive-by when students are reading to each other or silently reading the text. Whatever you do, don't set up an activity and then

retire to your desk doing paperwork until the bell goes. You can do paperwork, but every few minutes, take a spin around the room to monitor progress and make sure everyone is OK. This is especially important during testing. Shy students will not want to bother a teacher busy sitting behind her desk, but they will ask a question if she is doing a drive-by.

Drive-bys also let you step in early when a student is heading down the wrong path during an assignment or miniassessment. Immediate feedback is a critical part of learning. If you can catch a student making a mistake and guide him to correct it on the spot, you'll create a stronger learning opportunity than handing back the work a few days later. Be sure to *guide* rather than *tell* the students the answer. Instead, pepper them with questions that lead to the correct understanding. Some teachers find this idea of helping students correct themselves on a test quite controversial. Again, we need to go back to the fundamental question—*what are we trying to achieve?* If we want to ensure the student understands the material by the time they get to the state test, then this is an excellent strategy, because guiding students on the spot in the middle of an assessment is extremely effective. They are highly focused and engaged, and will remember the moment when they achieved a better understanding of the material.

Motivate

Take every possible opportunity to recognize, reward, and celebrate the positive. This is the key to creating happy, positive, polite middle school citizens. There are countless ways to reinforce positive behavior in your classroom. Here are 14 suggestions:

1. Smile

2. Mini-messages

3. Team tokens

4. Earn RECESS

5. Notice good days

6. The Golden Weiner award

7. Superhero awards

8. Schoolwide positive behavior

9. Punch cards

10. Karate belts

11. HOT tickets

12. Breakfast of champions

13. Homework on time chart

14. Brain bucks

Smile

When your students arrive scowling, make eye contact and smile. A smile softens a rough morning, lifts confidence, and reminds your students that, in this classroom, someone cares about them. You'll see frowns turning into smiles, eyes brightening, posture straightening, and steps becoming lighter. During class discussions, try to catch the eye of shy students and give them a reassuring smile. Their body language will speak volumes. They'll smile back, relax their shoulders, and start to enjoy the discussion.

Mini-Messages

Mini-messages are little private notes you slip secretly to individual students to reinforce positive behavior. A tiny note appears in their desk, from you, congratulating them on a specific positive act that you'd like to encourage. Perhaps they assisted you in preparing for an activity or helped another student. Perhaps they were kind to a new kid or have been making an extra special effort in class. Perhaps they came up with an exceptional answer.

Look for good behavior that is out of character, demonstrates effort, or you know the student is proud of. Make sure students know that you notice when they try hard and appreciate their hard work and thoughtfulness. Every student should receive at least one message throughout the year.

You can make mini-messages out of small pieces of paper or index cards. Some teachers decorate them or stamp *Well done!* on them. You can also buy "pocket praise" message cards from baudville.com. These are about the size of a matchbook when folded up and fasten closed. They come in an assortment of colors and sayings.

Don't mention the message to the student recipient. Let her decide how to acknowledge it. Some will keep it hidden. Others will have it out proudly on their desk. Some will come up and thank you. Others may slip you their own note in return!

Classroom Snapshot

One student received a mini-message that read, *See, I told you, you could do it!* During our state testing, she had it sitting out on her desk to boost her confidence.

Team Tokens and Punch Cards

Team tokens and punches reinforce appropriate teaming behavior. Create the punch cards for the first time after your class has decided together what a good functioning team looks and sounds like. These are just index cards—one per team—which your students decorate with their team name, icon, and cheer. They add *M*, *T*, *W*, *TH*, and *F* around the outside edges representing the days of the week, where you will hole punch. (Use a puncher that punches stars instead of holes if you're afraid your students will try to cheat). Thereafter, every time you change teams, the new team makes a new punch card.

At the beginning of the year, get your students to make the team tokens. Again, these are index cards decorated colorfully with the words *TEAM TOKEN* printed on them. When you see teams working hard or collaborating well, place a team token on their table, at the same time telling them *why* you are placing it there. At the end of the class or period, someone from the team brings up their tokens for you to punch their team punch card. When the teams swap over, those with a certain number of punches—get your students to nominate a fair amount—earn a reward. For example, root beer floats or a dip into the prize jar.

Earning RECESS

For self-contained classrooms, you can get your students to earn recess, as opposed to losing it. Each letter in the word *R-E-C-E-S-S* stands for four or five minutes of recess time, depending on how long you have in your school. Each day, your class starts fresh with a blank slate and NO RECESS. During the morning, students earn letters through positive behavior, for example, getting organized, completing work on time, working well as a team, or lining up quietly.

Using this concept not only helps your students remember what behavior is expected, it also makes you focus on the good things your students are doing—because you are actively looking for them. If you forget to give out letters, you can always have a big catch up moment. You might say, "Gosh, there aren't any letters up there. Let's think back over the hour. We sure had great participation from all of our groups! That earns us an *R*. Great questions were generated for that social studies game; that earns us an *E*.'"

If you're not seeing any good behavior, don't be tempted to take letters away. Instead, use the need to earn letters as an incentive for students to pick up their game. Rather than being cross, say very positively, "We need to earn some letters! I am on the lookout for organized teams, and teams who are working VERY hard!" Immediately, your students will refocus their attention and get back to work. Having the letters visible for everyone to see is a constant reminder of how well the class is doing that day.

On those glorious days when your students complete their responsibilities in record breaking time, give them extra letters! This means more recess time.

In the beginning, you can be extremely generous with your letter giving—you want your students to see how easy it is to earn letters with proper behavior. As the year progresses, you may use the letters less and less, because your students have learned what behaviors are expected in your classroom. Some years, they'll just fade away, you're your students won't even notice.

Of course, if your students forget how to behave—perhaps close to Christmas—you can bring back the R-E-C-E-S-S. All you need to do is say, "I think we forgot how to use our manners. Let's remind ourselves. We are going back to *earning* recess for the week."

Classroom Snapshot

I often hear my students encourage each other by saying, *Let's get organized and earn a letter*! That is where I can pipe in and add, *YES! That's the spirit; I like how this team is getting their homework and their checker pens out. That is what earns letters for the class!* Our current record is fifty minutes of recess earned.

Notice Good Days

Make good days stand out by complimenting your students before they leave and asking them to reflect on their achievements. You might say, "You did great today. I noticed lots of positive behavior.

What do you think you did well?" The conversation only needs to be for a minute. It might go like this:

Katelyn:	"Well, I think when we discussed the article, the class as a whole really participated providing evidence."
Teacher:	"Yes, I agree!"
Josh:	"We were all ready on time."
Teacher:	"I noticed that as well!"
Timmy:	"We worked as TEAMS rather than groups. We all contributed to the conversation . . . well, at least in our team anyway."
Teacher:	"I did notice that about your team. What about other teams, would you say everyone contributed to the conversation?"
Victoria for Team 5:	"Our team definitely had great conversations. We each found different evidence to support the question of the day!"
Teacher:	"I agree with all of you. It was a GREAT day today! You made my day sweet, so on your way out, grab yourself a sweet treat!"

The power here is in getting peers to notice positive behavior, not just the teacher. It reaffirms the importance of teaming for your students and helps to build a sense of community, where everyone understands what's required of them.

The Golden Weiner Award

Create a fun trophy from a cheap toy, which you can put on the table with the best behavior at any given moment. You can use a *Golden Weiner*, *Top Banana*, *Sacred Onion* or any other quirky trophy—perhaps your class mascot—that appeals to or has relevance for your students. Whenever you see good behavior, good answers, or great questions, the table gets the trophy. Sometimes, it may only land on the table for a minute, until another team scores it with another outstanding answer. On good days, it should bounce back and forth between tables like a ping-pong ball.

Don't keep score of who has the trophy for the greatest amount of time; it's just fun and games to see who can earn it back with hard work and creativity.

Classroom Snapshot

The Golden Weiner Award was born when I accidentally said, *I'm looking for organized teams, ready to move on . . . I'm looking for a weiner of a team!* It was so funny, we joked about it all day, and I went out that afternoon and bought a plastic weiner dog toy! From that point on when I saw teams going above and beyond, completing their responsibilities on time and without coerce, I would give them the now esteemed *WEINER AWARD*!

Superhero Awards

To increase student awareness of good behavior, introduce Superhero awards. These are peer-nominated awards earned when students do things for each other that go above and beyond the call of duty. When you tell your students that they can secretly nominate their peers for this Superhero award, make sure you discuss the sort of things *they* feel are worthy of this honor, so people understand how *heroic* they need to be.

Put some small, simple nomination tickets where students can easily access them. Then, when they want to nominate a classmate, they grab a ticket, fill it out, and give it to you. As soon as you receive a nomination ticket, take the first free moment you get and give the signal—a special bell or a sound effect. The student who completed the nomination stands up, announces the superhero and explains the great act of kindness that resulted in the nomination. The class claps, and the nominee chooses a superhero toy (buy several figures!) to sit at their place for the duration of the day. You can also toss the tickets into a jar for future drawings toward your school's positive behavior incentive.

This award system will make your students look at their peers in a different way. It also wakes some students up to the fact that they should step up a bit more. Typically, these are good students who sit quietly and get good grades. They are never a problem, but neither do they step up and help other people. This award is often the incentive they need to step out of their comfort zone and help another student.

Schoolwide Positive Behavior

If your principal is supportive, you can institute a schoolwide initiative to accentuate positive behavior, for individuals and classes. Teachers use colored tickets to record outstanding individual behavior (red) and exceptional class behavior (blue). At the end of each month, the whole school gathers for a quick ticket-drawing assembly. For example, in one school, ten student tickets are drawn, the first being the grand prize winner. The grand prize winner receives a school tote filled with school supplies as well as donated gift cards for local businesses. The subsequent nine receive bracelets that read *Exceeding Expectations*, and their names appear in the monthly newsletter. Five class tickets are drawn too. The first class wins a party of their choosing; the others receive ice cream coupons from the principal.

Punch Cards

At the start of each year, give each student a punch card. These are the size of a business card, with twenty stars, which get punched when the student achieves something. You can use punch cards to encourage any type of positive behavior—for example, reading a book, passing an accelerated reading test, completing a math assignment. Students achieving all twenty punches are officially in the Punch Club. This entitles them to a prize. If they are getting punches for reading, perhaps the prize could be one free book from the book club. Or you could schedule to have lunch with Punch Club members. Once a student fills a punch card, she receives a new one to start all over again!

These are excellent rewards for students who are hard to motivate because they can't easily see the end result. Having the visual reminder of how many activities they have to go is a great motivator.

Karate Belts

Karate belts are those popular rubber wrist bands that come in various colors. Choose six different colors for your students to work toward. For example, in reading, when a student reads four books he might receive his yellow belt, eight books might earn an orange belt, and so on. Once a student qualifies for a belt, use a special sound effect to signal this achievement, and with great fanfare, hand out the belt and give the recipient a huge round of applause.

You can keep your Karate Challenge standings outside your classroom on the wall. Give each belt a designated place on the wall to signify the standings, and get your students to make their own karate guy—perhaps clipart cut out with their picture on it. Each time they receive a belt, the student moves their guy to the appropriate belt area. Here the entire school can keep an eye on the challenge.

HOT Tickets

Homework on Time (HOT) tickets are superb motivators for students who struggle to get their homework in on time. The tickets go into a jar for a weekly drawing. You can make the drawing fun by rolling a die to see how many tickets will be drawn from the jar. Winning students receive a free homework pass or a trip to the prize drawer.

You can use HOT tickets for a variety of reasons. Perhaps some students have been wonderful bringing in their homework, so you want to reinforce this. Perhaps only a few students got their homework in on time, so you can reward them. The key is to be unpredictable. Students never know *when* you will give out HOT tickets.

Breakfast of Champions

Keep a log of the homework brought in complete and on time. Every nine weeks, invite those students who brought in every piece of homework during that time to attend a "Breakfast of Champions." This is a day when students come in twenty minutes before school starts for a breakfast provided by you. This could be as simple as donuts and milk. If allowed, budding chefs can bring in an electric skillet and scramble up some eggs.

Homework on Time (HOT) Chart

Create a chart to reward students for bringing in their homework. Whenever the entire class brings in their homework on time, stamp one of the boxes on the chart. As a class, determine what would be a fair target. You might want to start your goal at fifteen to twenty stamps. Whenever you reach your designated class goal—celebrate! Give your students a choice of reward, perhaps an *extra-day-to-do-homework coupon*, a *NO HOMEWORK coupon*, or new pencils or pens.

Brain Bucks

For those really difficult classes, use reward tickets that act as a currency in your class. Students receive these *brain bucks* for good behavior, class participation, or team togetherness. When they accumulate a certain number of bucks, students can use them to buy a prize. Typically, you don't need to use this type of reward system for very long. Eventually, you can wean your students off the tickets by slowing down how many you give out until, finally, the ticket flow stops. Once your class is behaving well without the tickets, make sure you occasionally reward great behavior with a movie, extra recess, or free time. Your students should get these treats, only when genuinely deserved and when they're least expecting them.

Classroom Snapshot

While correcting our midterm reading assessments, I noticed the entire sixth grade passed with either advanced or proficient scores. Elated at the 100% proficiency, I asked my principal if we could celebrate our success by having a "sixth-grade snow day." With his blessing, my colleague and I took the group outside for an hour to play and sled in the snow. They had never been so happy and appreciative as they were that day. These students are actually looking forward to our next big testing day!

Dealing With Discipline Issues

No matter how much you reinforce positive behavior, every so often you will still have to deal with discipline incidents. When this happens, talk calmly to the student away from the rest of the class—never raise your voice. Try to use *I* as opposed to *you*, which puts students on the defensive. For example, you might say, "I believe you can have a nicer tone of voice when you speak to your neighbor. I'm not sure I like what I am seeing. I wonder how we could improve this situation." This suggests to a student that the incident is a problem for the two of you to solve together, rather than a blame game. As a result, they are more likely to be honest, remorseful, and change their behavior.

When there is conflict between two students, make sure you get both sides of the story. Pull both parties out for a private conversation and start by saying to Student 1, "*I* understand there are differences between you and Student 2. I would like to hear your side of the story." Then ask Student 2 to share her perspective. If there are differences, you could say, "I hear some discrepancies between the two stories. Would you like to modify your story at all?" Often, students will make some clarifications and the truth comes out. Then you need to guide the students to work out their differences. You could ask questions such as, "How are we going to fix this? What should you have done? What do you think are the next steps for the two of you?"

Classroom Snapshot

Finding the positive not only creates a warm environment for the kids, but it also transforms my own state of mind as well. When I focus on my students' positive behaviors, I find I nitpick less and it actually gives *me* a much needed emotional boost. I know it sounds simple and trite, but finding that teeny-weeny little bit of goodness has a powerful effect on everyone in my classroom.

Key Points

- Learning stops when we shout at, humiliate, or punish our students.
- Instead, we need to demonstrate, facilitate, and motivate good behavior.
- Your attitude is contagious—model the behavior you want.
- Be specific about the behavior you expect—many students genuinely don't know what good behavior looks like.
- Find the itty-bitty bit of better behavior—you may have to look very hard!
- Ignore the size of their file—expect goodness and give students the benefit of the doubt.
- Give clear instructions and use engaging transitions.
- Praise and reward positive behavior all the time.

6

U-Turn Teaching in Action

This chapter looks at U-Turn teaching in action, demonstrating what it looks like when teachers take into account the guiding insights of brain-based learning. It starts with an intentional learning framework for ensuring students connect with, process, and understand new information. Then it offers a series of case studies to show how teachers can incorporate the U-Turn ideas in actual lessons, within specific content areas. Finally, it ends with a series of ideas for reviewing material in a variety of creative ways that your students will actually look forward to.

Intentional Learning Framework

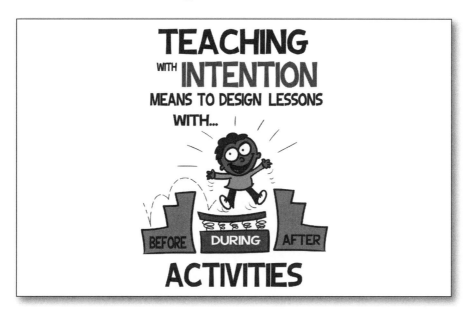

We know that, for the brain to learn, we cannot just keep pushing information into it. Learning is like eating. We get the best results from taking in small bites of information, chewing it to extract all possible understanding, and then digesting it so we retain this meaning as knowledge. Forcing information down our students' throats simply doesn't work. As teachers, we need to deliberately build into our lessons places where we make sure students:

- BITE: pique student curiosity and prompt them to access prior knowledge the new information will connect to—**before** the lesson
- CHEW: have multiple opportunities for students to process and manipulate new information—**during** the lesson
- DIGEST: ask students to demonstrate their new knowledge and give them strategies for placing it into long-term storage—**after** the lesson

BITE (before)

The following Bite activities serve three purposes. First, they make your students hungry to learn and question. If you can peak their curiosity and anticipation before a lesson, it makes your job 100 times easier, because your students will drive their own learning. Also, anticipation enhances alertness and releases feel-good chemicals like dopamine, epinephrine, and norepinephrine to support the learning process.

Second, they will help your students hook the new information into their prior knowledge, including reviewing the vocabulary needed to make connections with the upcoming ideas. This is important, because human beings organize new information around their previously developed schemata (networks of connected ideas). If your students don't connect new information with their existing ideas, it will quickly become lost. But if they connect it with a cluster of related existing ideas, they will find it easier to remember.

Third, the process of realizing that they already know a little bit about the new topic will give your students confidence that they can master it. Bringing information from past learning to the forefront of their minds allows students to predict upcoming content, with the sense of familiarity serving to further boost their confidence.

Note: Even if the learner has no prior experience with the topic, we still need to find a way to connect it with some known information—as demonstrated in the following activities.

Sample BITE Activities

Know Want Learned (KWL)

This well-known Bite activity is a quick, simple means of getting your students to both access prior knowledge and engage with the new topic. Ask them to fold a piece of paper in thirds and label the columns K/W/L:

1. KNOW—students list anything they already know, or think they know, about the upcoming topic.

2. WANT—students generate questions they have about the topic.

3. LEARNED—at the end of the lesson, students summarize their new knowledge.

If appropriate, during your lesson, students can come back to their chart and continue to generate additional questions based on what they have already learned.

5-Minute Math

KWL is hard to use in math. Instead, you can achieve the same outcomes with a five-minute activity or problem that previews the day's lesson. Create a 5-minute math chart by writing a problem on a piece of oaktag and placing it in a central location. Establish a routine where students know that, at the beginning of a math lesson, they simply need to have a go at the problem for a few minutes. Make sure they know it's just a little teaser of what's ahead. Tell them to just try it—not lament over it. Then, to begin your lesson, solve the problem, highlighting and linking the key strategies needed for the day.

For example, if the 5-minute math chart had *3x3x3* on it, you might say, "Ah, now that you see 3x3x3=27, we're going to kick it up a notch and take that understanding and connect it to this . . . 3 to the third power.

You can also use 5-minute math as a week-ahead preview. The idea is that students quickly have a go at a new problem—never taking more than 5 minutes—and then the teacher spends a couple of minutes demonstrating how to solve the problem. For example, if you are studying exponents next week, this Monday use your 5-minute math chart to introduce 3 to the third power. On Tuesday, introduce 2 to the fourth power, and so on. Generally, by Wednesday, many lightbulbs will have already clicked on, and about 75% of your class will get 5-minute math correct. Then, next week, when it's time to really dig into the content of exponents, your students will already have a basic understanding, enabling them to grasp more complex concepts quickly.

Review/Preview

This is another powerful routine. Establish six numbered stations/locations around the room for review/preview questions written on oaktag cards. Write one question or problem on the front of each card and the corresponding answers on the back. The first five cards cover review topics, based on your students' needs. Try to continually hit various skills and keep them fresh in your students' minds.

The sixth question previews today's new topic.

When your students come in and see the six cards hanging up in their stations, this is the cue for them to draw and number six boxes in their notebooks. Start them off by saying, "Table 1, you'll start at Problem 1, Table 2, you'll start at Problem 3 . . . and so on." Students then work at their own pace around the room solving the problems in their own time. They do not have to stay with their table group and can sit down once they are finished. Only allow five minutes for this activity.

When most students are sitting down, quickly go over the review questions. Only stop and work through problems if lots of students struggled with a particular question. Once you get to Problem 6, this is where your real lesson begins. Use the new problem and its answer to jump into the new topic.

For example, you might say: "OK, Problem 6. Is the sentence a run-on, declarative, fragment, or imperative? 'Before I go to the store to rent a movie.' The answer is . . . (flip the card) . . . fragment. This is where we are heading today, sentence fragments. Let's analyze this sentence and compare it to what we know about what sentences need."

Predict/Confirm

Give your students a handout about the main objectives of the upcoming unit of study.

PREDICT AND CONFIRM

Name: _____   Date: _____

Lesson/Unit: _____

Read the statements. Predict TRUE/FALSE and support your prediction with a complete sentence. After reading the selection, confirm your prediction.

Statement	Predict (You)	Confirm (Author)

Their task is to predict if the statement is true or false. This starts the thinking process. It also introduces your students to new vocabulary, ideas, and possible scenarios in the learning. At the end of the topic, your students can revisit the handout to see if their predictions were correct. To cement their learning, make sure they rewrite any false statements, using their new knowledge about the subject, to make them true.

Generate Questions

The brain loves questions. When posed with a question, it automatically seeks out an answer—accelerating learning. Take advantage of this innate need by asking your students, individually, or in teams, to generate a list of test questions based on the headings and pictures in the text for a lesson.

They can write the questions on index cards or chart paper. With index cards, when students find the answer as the class makes its way through the text, they can put the answer on the back. You can then use these generated questions and answers as review quiz resources.

Or, teams could write the questions on chart paper and post it around the room. In this case, other teams are challenged to answer the questions as the class progresses though the unit.

If some of the questions aren't answered by the text, this will prompt deeper research.

Plausible Paragraphs

Give your students a list of terms, names, or locations from the upcoming content. The list should also include terms from past units and lessons to help students make connections with existing knowledge. Challenge your students to use these terms to create a plausible paragraph covering what they think the chapter or lesson is about. When you start using this strategy, give your students a starter paragraph to fill in the gaps; for example, *I believe this lesson will be about _____, because I noticed _____, and I already know _____.*

After the lesson, students can revisit their paragraphs and correct or add information based on what they now know.

Association Game

As a class, brainstorm words associated with your new topic of study. Give your students the first couple of words and allow time for self-reflection before beginning the rapid-fire generation of associated terms. Make sure your students understand the concept of brainstorming. Tell them this is just to get their brains firing. There's no such thing as a stupid idea. Once the ideas start rolling, jot them down on the board as students jot them on scrap paper, creating a list of fifteen to thirty words. Put a clear time limit on the exercise—you could add drama by using a giant egg timer as part of the challenge: "We have until the sand runs out to generate at least fifteen words—let's go!"

Once your students have become adept at brainstorming associated terms as a class, you can move to brainstorming in teams. One fun option for teams is to ask students to rip scrap paper into bite-sized pieces. When the topic is announced, one person in the group (usually the leader) starts the brainstorming by saying a word, writing it down on the bite-sized paper, and tossing it into the middle of the table. The person on the right or left of the leader goes next, and so on around the group. After a set time, the group organizes the scraps into categories for use, such as mind mapping.

Alternatively, give each team a large piece of chart paper on which to write the results of their brainstorm. Afterwards, teams post their charts around the room. With sticky notes in hand, and when the music begins, students rotate to the next chart. If they see an idea that wasn't originally on their chart, they take that idea away with them on their sticky notes. Rotation continues every thirty to sixty seconds (keeping things quick) until they reach their starting point. Then the group can add their sticky notes to their original chart, making new connections.

Meaning Mix-Up

Quickly learning new vocabulary is vital to students' coming to grips with a topic, whether it's math, science, or social studies. Moreover, 90% of state assessments are based around key terminology. Your students may know how to jump through every state-standard hoop asked of them, but if they don't know the appropriate terminology, they will still fail the test.

Many teachers understand this, but try to teach vocabulary by asking students to write down new words and their definitions in a journal. For middle schoolers in particular, this is boring, ineffective, and a HUGE waste of time.

Leak, ooze, dribble	Identify, detect, recognize	Deadly, fatal, dangerous	Request, demand	Meeting point, assembly point
Eat greedily, gulp down	Intercept	Interrupt, cut off, catch	Rendezvous	Seep
Diagnose	Lethal	Plea	Devour	

The meaning mix-up offers you a far more engaging alternative. Before starting a new reading selection, simply fill in a table with the seven to ten new vocabulary words most vital for understanding, along with their corresponding synonyms (see example table, above).

Once you have read over the terms and synonyms as a class, ask your students to cut out the boxes and try to match the vocabulary word boxes to the appropriate synonym boxes. It's a trial and error activity that gets them deeply engaged, thinking, and using context clue skills. Moreover, it introduces them to try various synonyms they may have never considered using in place of the given term.

When a student thinks he has the terms matched up correctly, let him know which ones are correct, so he can set those off to the side. Let students go back for a second or third attempt, but don't let them struggle for very long. This is just an introductory activity. You're going to work with the words shortly, so meanings will soon become clear. When the first student at each table has sorted the words correctly, put him in charge. Now, when students at this table complete their sort, they can call on the student in charge to check for accuracy.

Once sorted, your students can paste the cards into vocabulary notebooks, subject journals, or mini-file folders. Middle schoolers love mini-file folders (or indeed anything very big or very small), which are about half the size of a standard manila file folder.

Picture/Text Feature Walk

Before diving into a new text, complete a *picture walk* where students simply take thirty seconds to scan the pictures, diagrams, headings, pull-out boxes, and graphs in the text. Ask them to be ready to tell you what they noticed, what it made them think of, and what questions they have. If they want to, they can jot down facts or questions on an index card.

Classroom Snapshot

Lindsey:	*It appears, based on the map on page 157 that Canada has a vast array of landforms like mountains, valleys, plateaus.*
Teacher:	*Good, very specific Lindsey. Who else? Alexis?*
Alexis:	*I noticed that the highest mountain is 15,000 feet above sea level! That sounds high! I wonder if the U.S. has any mountains that high.*
Teacher:	*Good question. Jot that down, and we'll look that up later.*

This discussion can continue as long as you wish. All the time, students are generating their own questions and making their own connections. They are also linking concrete images with a potentially abstract concept, greatly assisting understanding (Tate, 2003, p. 45). This is especially important for visual learners, but all your students will benefit from these visual hooks, on which they can hang the new information.

Treasure Chest Intrigue

Artifacts offer another great way to link an abstract concept with something real. You can create curiosity and drama by pulling items out of a dusty old treasure chest. Just the sight of the chest will make your students sit up and take notice.

Of course, other containers work just fine. For example, when studying the Bay of Fundy on the Gulf of Maine, you could fill a five-gallon bucket full of items you would need or find if you took a trip there—perhaps boots, starfish, shells, and small shovels. Before the lesson, allow each student to touch and examine each article. Then, ask them to predict what the area must be like, what a visitor might find. Once you start reading about the Bay of Fundy, you'll find students constantly making connections. They will suddenly say, "Oh, that's why you had the boots in there!" All the time, they are making more connections, improving their recall of the new topic.

CHEW (during)

In the lesson itself, we must build in activities that give students time to process the new information by talking or thinking about it or manipulating it in some way. This requires us to STOP teaching and allow our students to create meaning from the new material. Only after they have finished *chewing* can we serve more information.

Remember, the brain is poor at sustaining continuous high levels of attention. Once your students reach their attention limit (ten minutes at the most for middle schoolers), any information you give after this point will be lost. Pushing more and more information into your students' brains virtually guarantees a lack of retention.

Instead, we need to build in processing—either internal (self-reflection) or external (students working together to manipulate the information).

Before we look at different processing activities, it's important to understand what this means for lesson design. Essentially, it means we need to give our students a CHUNK of information, and then let them CHEW on it before giving them the next chunk. So, if your students have been *listening* to you talk for several minutes, then you need to insert an activity using a different modality, such as talking or writing, to allow consolidation.

Sample Lesson Design

CHUNK Step 1—the teacher explains and draws on the whiteboard the new concept of food chains. Students take notes. (ten minutes)

CHEW Step 2—the students are asked to reread their notes, fix any mistakes, box new words in color. (one to two minutes)

CHUNK Step 3—partners read the next section of the text together and add to their notes. (ten minutes)

CHEW Step 4—students stand and meet a different person. They compare notes, add any missing information. (two to three minutes)

CHUNK Step 5—the teacher discusses the third portion of the concept as students add to their notes.

Sample CHEW Activities

The following activities (from multiple sources) will help your students to chew on the new information. In the process, the learner will think about, visualize, and summarize information. At the same time, you will be able to assess students' understanding, allowing you to adjust your instruction to their level of comprehension.

Simple 1 Minute CHEWS

- Stop and reread notes
- Reread notes and highlight key terms
- Box key terms and shade them in with colored pencil
- Draw icons/images for key terms

Think/Pair/Share (Lyman, 1981, p. 132)

Find natural stopping points in your reading or lecture material—making sure you don't talk for more than ten minutes. Then ask your students to THINK about a given question. For example, "How would you describe the character's feelings at this point in the story?" Give them twenty to thirty seconds and then ask students to turn to the nearest person and share their thinking with that partner. To hold students accountable, occasionally ask what a partner's answer was, or how their partner's answer was different or similar to their own.

Thought Jots (Dodge, 2005, p. 58)

After ten minutes of lecturing, stop and ask your students to draw a simple stop sign in their notebooks. Then ask a question related to the content, and give your students thirty seconds to *jot* down their response in their notes. Or ask them to jot down a possible test question based on the new information, or several facts they want to tell their family about this topic.

Stop/Jot/Share

This combines the above two ideas. When you stop lecturing, your students jot down their thoughts, before sharing them with a partner from across the room—an excellent excuse to stretch their legs.

Doodle Your Noodle

This is similar to Thought Jots, but uses images instead of words. After ten minutes of lecture, students draw illustrations beside their notes. This processing activity is extremely helpful for visual and kinesthetic learners.

Partner Walk

Especially after a heavy piece of content or a long period of sitting, allow students to pair up and take a short walk to the end of the hallway and back, discussing a content-related question. When they return, they must report their partner's point of view on the discussed question.

'Sticky'- Point

At a designated stopping point, ask a question based on the text and get your students to write their answers on a sticky note. They then must jump back into the text to investigate, locate, and ultimately stick their answer near the evidence that supports that answer.

Talking Text Tags

Give student pairs question sheets with a stopping page and paragraph number as well as a question to answer.

Example:

> **Stop** page 86
>
> **Paragraph** 5
>
> **Question:** What can you learn about the character based on how he handles the conflict?

Partners read through the selection, stop at the appropriate points, and write their answers down on sticky notes. They then *tag the text* by placing the sticky note where the evidence is located. Then when asked, they can quickly go back to their text tags, read their answers, and support them with evidence from the selection.

Note Taking (3 Columns)

Column 1	Column 2	Column 3
Vocabulary	Definitions and Notes	Visual Representation of the Concept

Middle schoolers need a lot of modeling when it comes to note taking. As you make your way through a lesson, stop and discuss what is important to remember—and take notes about—in that section of the lesson. Use the three column model above to help your students record, understand, and remember new vocabulary. Fill in the first two columns as you go through. Then, at the end of each section, get your students to go back and add visual representations of that information. At first, you'll have to be very explicit when you show them how to add visuals. You might say:

> When I think about the goods that America exports, we said we wanted to remember that America is the largest producer of corn in the world, and it exports 20% of its corn crop. So I'm going to write 20% in the third column and make the zero into a cob of corn to help me remember that. We also mentioned that more of our exports go to Canada than any other country. What image or icon could we add to our notes to help us remember this?

DIGEST (after)

Make sure you leave enough time at the end of the period for this final consolidation step, where students will solidify their learning. In this step, we give our students opportunities to reflect on and demonstrate their new knowledge through summarizing, consolidating facts, discussing new ideas, and responding to questions. Such activities will help your students to transfer new information into long-term storage.

In fact, Digest may be the most critical phase of learning, yet it's often the least utilized because teachers run out of time. We must deliberately build in time for this vital step if we want our students to form solid memories of the content.

Additionally, and most importantly, the process of digesting their new learning is extremely satisfying for your students. They get to see that they did understand and can remember the information, leading to the proverbial, *Yessss, I did it!* moment. Never underestimate the power of this moment. If learning makes students feel good about themselves, they will come back for more. Imagine a room full of students who are keen to learn and excited about your next lesson!

Sample Digest Activities

Ticket Out/Exit Cards (Dodge, 2005)

Before students leave, they must complete a *ticket out*—putting their answers to a few assessment questions on a named index card, before depositing it in a basket or bucket. The questions should be quick and assess the core objectives of the day's lesson. For example, in math, you might set a few basic problems or, in English, you might ask your students to write a sentence or two demonstrating the use of coordinating conjunctions. Then you can quickly and easily evaluate who has grasped the main concepts of the lesson—separating the cards into piles of students who have and have not understood the lesson. If half the class is struggling, the next day, you can pair students up for peer tutoring. Or, if only one or two didn't get it, you can talk to them individually during class.

3–2–1 Ticket Out

Students fill out an index card stating:

3—things they learned today

2—questions they have about the material

1—personal response to the material (e.g., eye opening, startling, boring, interesting, confusing, provocative, made them think about . . .)

Again, you can see who understood the concepts, where there are still misunderstandings or questions, and also how the students felt about the material.

You can pull these back out the next day as a quick review and to set the stage for the next bit of information. Without naming names, you can highlight accurate statements that were well thought out, correct any misconceptions, and share the most thought provoking questions. To solidify understanding still further, read out statements and ask the class if the statements are true or false. If a statement is false, ask for a volunteer to correct the statement in her own words. Then ask a few of the generated questions, focusing on the ones that you have already answered in class, but were obviously missed by someone. This way, you can make sure the whole class is up to speed.

Recap and Represent! (Dodge, 2005)

This allows students to digest their new learning in a visual format. You can use the form as a daily summation during a particular unit. At the end of the unit, the form becomes a review and study tool.

RECAP AND REPRESENT!	
Term/Main Idea/Question	*Recap in Writing or Sketch My Schema*
Date:	
Date:	
Date:	
Date:	
Date:	

Quick Write (Dodge, 2005)

A quick write is a timed writing assignment, generally one to five minutes, based on the content just covered. Students are given a question to respond to for the given amount of time. For example, "What challenges did the character face in her childhood?" or "How is the selection similar to your own life?" or simply be asked to summarize the content. Afterwards, students can then exchange papers with a partner, stand and share what they wrote with a partner, or even add important details to a partner's page. Encourage your students to use new vocabulary in their quick writes. You could also use this technique periodically throughout a long lecture. After a few minutes of talking, pause and allow time for a quick write before moving on.

Mind Map

Mind-mapping, invented by Tony Buzan (1996), is a complex graphic organizer that allows students to tap into prior learning, think creatively, analyze new information, and use visual images to represent abstract concepts. The idea is that note taking with words only limits learners' ability to see the whole picture. In a mind map, by attaching visuals to the words, students are able to synthesize and more easily remember the entire concept. The key is for students to make the mind map themselves and create personal visual reminders. The images don't have to be brilliant—just memorable.

Directions

1. BRAINSTORM ideas related to the central topic.

2. DRAW a picture in the center of the paper representing the concept. For example, if studying Native Americans, possibly a representation of a teepee could be used as the central image. (The image should be quite small to allow room for subsequent drawings and additions to the map.)

3. DRAW simple icons (pictorial images) randomly around the center to represent each idea on the list.

4. CONNECT the ideas using images such as dotted lines, chain links, lightbulbs, lightning bolts, arrows, or anything representing the topic.

5. ENCOURAGE students to limit words and to use color to add dimension and impact.

Here's the Answer; What's the Question?

Instead of using a worksheet filled with questions and blanks for answers, do the opposite. Hand out a worksheet with only the answers, and space for the students to write in the corresponding question. When using this activity for the first time, make it easy by placing small coin envelopes containing the questions around the room. Partners walk around the room, open the envelopes, and decide which question belongs to which answer. They then write the question from the slip of paper onto the line underneath the correct answer, before putting the question slip back into the coin envelope and moving on to the next one. Next time, simply ask the students to generate their own questions to the given answers.

Simple Sort

This activity allows students to sort out their ideas, while allowing you to help them focus on the key assessment skills and terms. The sort sheet includes categories, subcategories, terms, and key ideas from selections taught and being tested (see example).

Example of a Simple Sort Sheet on Water Ecosystems

Saltwater Ecosystems	Swamps	Ponds	Marshes
Very little sunlight	**Freshwater Ecosystems**	Prevents coastal flooding	**Ocean Zones (shallowest–deepest)**
Open-ocean zone	Calm waters	Intertidal zone	Streams
Most productive ecosystem	**Deep Ocean Water**	Near-shore zone	**Estuaries**

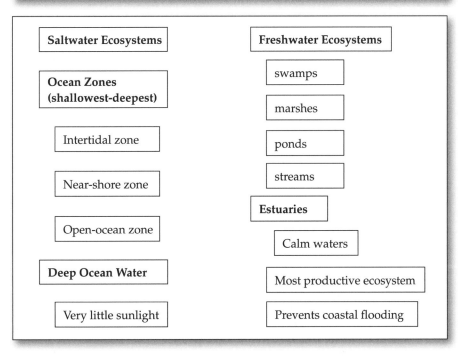

After reading and discussing the selection, ask your students to cut out the squares, and sort the information according to the new information, and glue them onto a piece of construction paper. Help your students get started by bolding the headings. As you walk around and watch students sorting their information, you can quickly assess their understanding of the material. Afterwards, ask your students to add pictures or icons to help them visualize the information, creating study guides for upcoming tests.

ABC Brainstorm

Ask your students to fold a large piece of chart paper in half, long-ways, and write the letters *A* through *M* down the left hand column, and the letters *N* through *Z* on the fold. Students then brainstorm words and phrases from the unit topic that start with the letters of the alphabet. For example, if we were studying *U-Turn Teaching*, one may look like this:

A—Always up!	N—Note taking
B—Brainstorming	O—Open communication
C—Chat and check	P—Positives run the room

To take this another step further, make it a timed activity, say five minutes, and then post their charts around the room. If the groups cannot get all of *A* through *Z* complete, use a carousel activity where students walk around to each chart and get ideas for filling in their blank letters.

Word Summary Pyramids

Challenge your students to create word summary pyramids using one-word, two-word, three-word, four-word, and five-word summaries underneath each other.

Example: One-Word Summary—Fractions

Fractions
Denominators, numerators
Find common factor
Simplify, divide top/bottom

Artifact Box

Instead of using this to introduce your lesson, ask your students to create an artifact box of items that represent the unit of study just completed. For example, a unit of decimals might yield an artifact box containing a baseball card (batting average), coins, Dow Jones stock exchange clipping from the newspaper, a box of macaroni (the weight is listed in decimals), a picture of an odometer, Matchbox car (NASCAR standings), stopwatch, or scale. This helps students to connect what they are learning to the real world.

Murals

After a brief overview of a topic, send your students off to dive deep into a week-long study on a particular theme. While they are researching, give each group of three to five students a long sheet of bulletin board paper, about five to six feet in length, on which to produce a mural. As they create these murals, you can monitor their understanding by looking at their use of visuals as well as listening to their conversations. You can also use murals for vocabulary instruction. Ask your students to create a mural incorporating as many of their words as possible, perhaps in conversations between the characters in their murals or showing the definition as a labeled pictorial representation. This activity is extremely effective, but don't wear it out. Using it once a semester is appropriate.

Give One-Take One

Teams are given an allotted amount of time to brainstorm and list words and phrases related to the topic just covered, and then hang their charts around the room. With music playing, as a team they move to the next chart paper. They read what is already there, add an idea using sticky notes, and then take an idea to add to their own chart paper.

Develop Questions

Ask your students to generate three questions and answers on index cards based on the daily lesson. These can be used to quiz other tables or their own tablemates. If used as a game for the entire class, ask students to gauge their question from easy to hard and assign it appropriate points. So, an easy question might earn 1 point, a hard one 5 points.

Journal/Diary Entry

Journaling allows students to reflect upon and process information, connect the information to their own lives, and write personal opinions about the content. In the early days of journaling, use simple entry starting with, *Today I learned* . . .

Then, use more thought-provoking starting points, *This makes me think about . . .* or *This information is important because . . .* You don't have to mark the journals or correct the grammar; simply scan them for basic understanding.

Draw It!

Ask your students to draw representations of whatever they are learning, no matter how abstract. For example, drawings can help students remember different, but similar sounding, spelling endings (for example, *-er, -or,* and *-ar*). Take the word *prisoner.* To help your students remember it ends in *-er,* draw a giant *e* on their paper. Using the *e* as the starting point, draw around it to create the meaning of the word. For example, in this scenario, the *e* would become a person locked in a prison.

Drama

Similarly, make the fullest possible use of drama (acting, singing, rapping, miming) in every single subject area.

- Act out vocabulary definitions, math rules, or property of matter.
- Become sentence types, pioneers, parts of speech, math problems, number lines, or characters in a book.
- Develop and sing songs/raps about mean, median, and mode, the four types of sentences, or historical events.

LESSON 1: READING DETECTIVES

Issue: My class was bored by the worksheet/oral discussion approach of the basal reading program. Most of my students are not auditory learners, and they soon tuned out all the oral discussion about the text. Reading and discussion time was met with groans, leaving me with a room full of reluctant learners.

U-Turn idea: The reading skills the basal program aims to teach can be aligned with detective work: you have to search for the author's purpose; you have to translate figurative language (clues) and summarize your findings. I decided we would become *reading detectives.*

Translating the curriculum: I replaced the worksheet/discussion activities with a *case file* developed around the basal story as well as my state standards. Students work on these case files with partners, with the activities in the case files prompting them to talk about the story and dig deep into the text.

Each case file has a number of standard activities to instill core skills:

- Genre boxes
- Author's purpose
- Point of view fingerprints (with clues)
- Figurative language
- One-minute fluency reads
- Vocabulary activities
- Story-specific activities based around the general story objective, perhaps looking at cause and effect, plot, and character analysis.

Case File Sample Activities

Use COLORED PENCIL to color in the appropriate box to indicate the genre of this story.

Realistic Fiction	Science Fiction	Historical Fiction	Fantasy	Folktale
Biography	Autobiography	Nonfiction	Mystery	Poetry

What is the AUTHOR'S PURPOSE for writing this piece? *Shade in the correct box.*

P	To **persuade** you to take up baseball.
I	To **inform** you about a true story about a girl who meets challenges.
E	To **explain** how to hit a fast pitch.

This story is written in _____ POINT OF VIEW

First Person

Third Person

CLUES: "I" and "We"   CLUES: "He," "She," "It," "They"

Equipment

- Case files
- Detective jackets and hats (I found some in the consignment store and asked parents for donations in my letter home)
- Identification badges

Procedure

1. Discussion: Set up the activity by discussing how reading is essentially like being a detective or CSI agent. Explain that, when we read, often we have to become a detective to solve the mystery of the author's purpose.

2. Preparation: Construct tool kits to support student investigations—envelopes filled with highlighters, colored pencils, sticky notes, pocket pads, and a mini magnifying glass—everything a good reading detective would need to identify and mark specific text features.

3. Transition: Establish some trigger music—perhaps, the theme from CSI, Pink Panther, or Dragnet. Tell your students that, when they hear this music, it's their cue that they have a case to solve. They need to put on their coats, gather their tool kits and case files, and meet you in the middle of the room to begin the undercover operation.

4. Execution: As a group, build the background on the story; do picture walks to prepare for your reading, develop vocabulary, and introduce the main skill of the day. From this point, you can send your students in pairs to find evidence of the daily skill and begin to read the weekly story or article.

Results

I covered all of my state standards with a month to spare, and my state reading assessment scores have been 96–100% proficient respectively each year using this detective/case files method.

Perhaps more importantly, my students were engaged and excited by the activity. They begged to "wear their coats and do detective work." There were no more groans—the class truly loved reading and investigating.

LESSON 2: MEASUREMENT CRIME SCENE

Issue: Across the board, our school's measurement scores on the state assessments were too low. My principal challenged the entire staff to make this section in the curriculum stick. I was aware that, in previous years, my students had struggled because the lines on a ruler are so tiny. Many students had a hard time figuring out what each line represented, and therefore would measure incorrectly. The traditional approach of measuring a few items and drawing a few lines had failed to translate into a practical skill.

U-Turn idea: I realized that, to become proficient at measuring with a ruler, my students would need lots of practice—far more than they were getting. I needed an activity that would keep them engaged and motivated to measure many, many different types of items. Knowing how much they loved becoming reading detectives, I decided to create crime scenes, where students could measure the items left behind by criminals.

Translating the curriculum: We exchanged the traditional worksheet activities for a two-part lesson. On Day 1, we learned how to measure. On Day 2, we entered crime scenes where students ended up measuring forty different items.

Equipment (Day 1)

- Giant six-foot ruler—a replica of your state assessment ruler.
- 3x replicas laminated—one for each student.

Equipment (Day 2)

- Tool kits (e.g., pencil boxes filled with measuring tape, rulers, pencils)
- Detective jackets
- Forty items to measure (each crime scene has ten items; these are just printed-off pictures that were each made to measure to the nearest ¼, ½, or ⅛ of an inch.)
- Plastic tablecloth or rug to use as an area on which to place the items
- Crime scene tape—found in Halloween stores or hardware stores
- Measurement packets
- Criminal posters
- Measurement data forms

Procedure

Day 1

1. *Group discussion:* Introduce the six-foot ruler to discuss the concept of measuring. As a class, discuss what each line represents. Ask students to run up and touch the ruler where they think a line represents a 1/4, 1/2, or 1/8 of an inch, for example.

2. *Individual practice:* Hand out their personal giant rulers. The whole point here is not to measure, but to make sure your students know what each line represents. Ask your students to use an expo marker to indicate different lines. For example, you might call out the measurement 2 3/8, and your students have to draw a line on the 2 3/8 line of their ruler. Then, you quickly scan the room to see if everyone has the correct line marked, and continue to demonstrate on the giant classroom ruler. Continue this process until you're confident each student has mastered the basic concept.

Day 2

1. *Preparation:* Set up four crime scenes with tape and place ten items inside each one on a rug or mat. Place a sign on the classroom door indicating *Crime Scene—Official Personnel Only . . .* and keep the door shut.

2. *Discussion:* Greet your students at the door, holding all of their detective coats. Explain to them there are four crime scenes within the classroom that need to be evaluated and solved. When everyone has put on his coat, enter the room and take a peek. Then, sit in your meeting place and discuss the procedure for evaluating each crime scene.

3. *Transition:* Play investigating music.

4. *Execution:* Groups of four students visit each scene one group at a time. Each group has to visit each crime scene. At each scene, they measure ten items, as well as the rug or mat the items are laid upon. They must measure the items to the nearest 1/8 of an inch, measure the area and perimeter of the rugs, and use their findings to fill in their crime scene form. This form is programmed like a puzzle, meaning it is designed in a manner where once they find a particular measurement or answer, they locate that measurement or answer on the crime

scene form, and it then corresponds to a particular letter. Put together, these letters spell out the name of the criminal for that area, such as Edith Eighth, Fred the Fourth, or Ida Inch. In addition, if a group finishes solving their scene before another is complete, they have a measurement packet to work on as they wait.

Results

Not only were the students totally engaged in the learning, they passed this portion of the state assessments with 100% proficiency! Having to measure forty real items truly gave them the practice and skill they needed to perform well in the test.

My valuable discoveries owe more to **patient attention** than any other talent ...

Isaac Newton

LESSON 3: OLYMPIC RACE

Issue: To get math skills to stick permanently, students need continual practice. However, my students were bored of the continual need to review. I knew that, to keep them engaged in practicing math, I needed a different approach.

U-Turn idea: My students were following the winter Olympics, so I decided to align math problems with this topical area of interest. I designed a giant Olympic game board for the class to build, with the idea that student pairs would move their playing pieces with each correct computation of their review problems.

Translating the curriculum: I cherry-picked review problems in topics that I knew my students were struggling with, for example, reducing fractions and changing mixed numbers into decimals. These became the challenges pairs had to overcome to move their pieces around the board.

Equipment

- Six to eight feet of bulletin board paper
- Printed pictures of Olympic athletes competing
- Playing pieces (I used little icons that match different sports, i.e., figure skater, bobsledder, skier, etc. and copied two each on heavy card stock)
- Lunch bags—as many bags as there are stops on the Olympic trail
- Various review problems and answer keys
- Sheet that will hold the answers
- Gold, silver, bronze plastic metals (optional)
- Sports drink and energy bars (optional)

Procedure

1. *Preparation:* As a class, use the bulletin board paper to create a route or game board that your students will move their game pieces on, with about fifteen stopping points. Make each stopping point on the board a different sport (the luge track, bobsledding area, the hockey rink). If appropriate, you can actually use the real Olympic map as a template. At each stopping point, we glued pictures of well-known Olympic competitors from that particular sport.

Label the lunch bags with different sports corresponding to the answer slots on their answer sheets. The idea is, if a pair grabs the bobsledding bag, they have to solve the problem and place their answers under the bobsledding heading on their answer sheet.

2. *Discussion:* As a group, talk your students through the rules of the game.

3. *Execution:* Pairs of students are given matching game pieces. When the music starts, students grab a lunch bag and begin solving a problem inside it. When they think they have it solved completely and correctly, they bring it to the teacher for checking. If the answer is correct, they can move their game pieces to the next sporting event. If it is incorrect, they have to work it out again until it is correct. You can monitor students' progress on the game board with the corresponding correct sections on their answer sheet. The first three pairs who make it to the end win gold, silver, and bronze metals. At the end, when everyone has completed the Olympic race, celebrate with a medal ceremony (with optional cups of sports drink and pieces of energy bar!)

Results

My students reviewed all the concepts they had been struggling with, while having a great time. As a benefit, I was able to see and individually help those students having difficulty with particular concepts.

LESSON 4: THIRD-PERSON PERSPECTIVE BINOCULARS

Issue: After discussing third-person omniscient and third-person limited perspective various times, as well as giving and finding examples in the text, my students still weren't grasping the idea of how third-person could be made into omniscient and limited.

U-Turn idea: I needed to find a connection between these abstract concepts and concrete ideas my students would be familiar with. How could I get them to understand the idea of perspective? I decided we would differentiate between the two concepts by using the following analogy:

> **Third-person limited—telescope**: The reader is limited to only seeing into the main character's head (a one lens/one perspective)

> **Third-person omniscient—binoculars**: Readers get to see all character's thoughts and feelings (two lenses/greater perspective)

Translating the curriculum: I didn't replace the entire curriculum; I just added to it. I introduced the concept of first and third person through the case files, but as we developed our knowledge base and understanding, I added to the third-person perspective by getting my students to create telescopes and binoculars to represent the two perspectives of third person, thus solidifying understanding.

Equipment

- Colored construction paper (8 x 10 and 8 x 17)
- White paper
- Colored pencils
- Definitions of third-person limited and omniscient posted
- Glue or tape

Procedure

Discussion

1. Explain the differences between first- and third-person perspective, focusing on the idea that third person can be divided into two other forms, limited and omniscient. Give examples from the text.

2. Explain to the students that to help them remember the difference between limited and omniscient, they will build binoculars and telescopes.

3. Explain that the telescope represents third-person limited, because as the reader, you can only see into the mind of the

main character. Therefore, there is only one lens and only one person present in our view finder.

4. Explain that binoculars represent omniscient, the ability to see into many characters' thoughts, hence the two lens and various people within our view finders.

Execution

1. Take the 8 x 17 construction paper, roll and tape it into a long tube.

2. On separate white construction paper, trace the circumference of the end of the telescope, making the eventual viewfinder of the telescope.

3. After cutting out the circle (lens), draw a figure (main character) and a thought (speech bubble) of what the character would say or think. This will represent the idea that readers can only see into the mind of the one main character.

4. After the scene is created on the lens, tape it onto the end of the telescope.

5. Label the outside of the telescope: *Third-person LIMITED*

6. Roll and tape two 8 x 11 pieces of construction paper into tubes and adhere together.

7. Tape a piece of 3 x 4 piece of construction paper over the two rolls to hold them together like binoculars. Label this: *Third-person OMNISCIENT.*

8. Trace two lenses from the circumference of the tubes, and tape to the ends.

9. Draw various characters and their thought perspectives to the main problem or dilemma of the story.

Results

By creating these reminders, the students immediately understood the difference between third-person limited and omniscient. I also used the telescopes and binoculars for review. I would say, "Pick up the device that shows when the author writes in a way that we know ALL characters' feelings; it is_____." My students then picked up their binoculars, and pretended to peer into them, allowing me to see instantly if they picked up the correct implement, and thus that they knew the difference.

LESSON 5: "CORRECT THOSE SENTENCES" GAME SHOW

Issue: While I have loved using and found great benefits from the Daily Language Review (DLR) from Evan-Moor for years, I found most of my students were uninterested and unengaged in the correcting process, which to me was the most important step. I needed to find a way to get all students excited, eager, and engaged in the correcting process of these daily reviews.

U-Turn idea: Instead of using oral correction, I developed a game that would achieve the same objective, while keeping everyone engaged and motivated.

Translating the curriculum: Instead of using oral correction, we put the incorrect sentences on the board to correct in a game show context. Students can only participate in the game show if they complete and correct the DLR on time.

Equipment

- Daily Language Review by Evan-Moor (or any other product that has various problems with mistakes to correct.)
- Colored pencils/pens (as correcting pens)
- Noise maker (I use Sound F/X by Trainers Warehouse) (www.trainerswarehouse.com)
- Plastic microphone
- Name cards
- Game show music (I actually use the theme from the show *Mork and Mindy*)
- Poster with editing marks

Procedure

1. Give students a DLR to complete as morning work. They must complete it by a specified time to participate in the game.

2. Write sentences from the DLR on the board, as found on the worksheet.

3. Choose one student to become game show host of the day. They will be the one holding the microphone and asking the participants what they did to the sentence.

4. Draw three students' names. They will be the first three to go up to the board to correct an error in the sentence.

5. Student 1 approaches the sentence, using editor's marks, he corrects one mistake he's found. He heads to the host and tells the audience what he corrected and why.

6. As Student 1 is telling the audience, Student 2 is simultaneously correcting another error found in the sentence.

7. After three students have gone, draw an additional three students to correct errors.

8. Continue this process until all errors are found and fixed within the sentences.

9. The students who remain in their seats circle the corresponding errors they hopefully corrected on their own papers. If they did not catch the error on their own, they are expected to correct the error at that moment.

Example

Given this sentence: john rhonda and camille rides the bus two school this morning

It may sound something like this. . .

Teacher:	*And the host today is* . . . (drum roll) . . . *Celina!* (applause and Celina grabs the microphone and heads to the front of the room.)
Teacher:	*The first three contestants today on* . . .
Audience:	(shouts) CORRECT THOSE SENTENCES! *Are* . . . (drum roll) . . . *Carly, Jacob, and Adam!* (applause)

"Mork and Mindy" theme music begins playing in the background as all three students head to the board. Carly is first up and corrects a mistake in the sentence and heads over to the hostess.

Hostess:	So, Carly, tell me what you did.
Carly:	I added a period to the end of the sentence because it is a declarative sentence.
Teacher:	(Using the Sound F/X toy sounds the correct sound.) Ta Da!

That signals to Carly that she is correct and can head back to her seat. (Audience applauds and circles the correction on their own

DLR). Jacob is the second participant to approach the board and corrects an error.

Hostess: So, Jacob, what did you do?

Jacob: I changed two to too in the sentence, because they didn't mean the number two.

Teacher: (Sounding the F/X buzzer) Buzz, buzz, buzz! That is partially incorrect. (Students in the audience are frantically waving their hands in the air, ready to assist Jacob. But first, Jacob must attempt to correct his mistake. If he cannot, he is permitted to call S.O.S. for assistance.)

Jacob: (After looking at the sentence for a moment) I don't know what I did wrong. S.O.S. Ben. (Ben scurries up to the board and corrects Jacob's error.)

Hostess: Ben, what did you do?

Ben: I changed Jacob's too to a to because the too Jacob used was to refer to something like too many.

Teacher: (Sounds the Ta-da, to show Ben is correct; to hold Jacob accountable, so he just doesn't always give up) *Jacob, what did Ben do?"*

Jacob: *Ben changed the number* two *and made it* to, *because that's what we use when we mean* go to.

Note: some of the best learning occurs when the participants make errors and students frantically vie for a chance to correct their peers. Make sure the game is played in a fun and nonthreatening way that does not embarrass students. It only works if you've set up, *right from the beginning*, that in your class mistakes are good because we learn from them.

Results

This game always results in total participation and engagement, as well as my students' gaining a deeper understanding of the concepts covered. The keys are getting the students to explain why they corrected the error and making sure the whole thing is played for laughs. Because the tone is very light, students are prepared to take risks and don't mind hearing the incorrect buzzer. Instead, they laugh, go back to the board, and have another go or call for assistance.

LESSON 6: CORNER SENTENCE TYPES

Issue: Even after years of spiral curriculum offered by our basal series, numerous discussions and worksheets later, my students STILL couldn't identify the four different types of sentences.

U-Turn idea: With my growing knowledge of different memory techniques, it dawned on me that there are four types of sentences, and four corners in my classroom. I decided to use physical location to help my students remember the four types of sentences.

Translating the curriculum: I replaced the usual drill and kill worksheet approach the basal reading method recommended it with activities that would lay down various memory pathways: rhyming, location, and positive emotion.

Equipment

- Construction paper
- Markers/colored pencils

Procedure

1. *Discussion*: Discuss, review, and look at the four different types of sentences, making sure students have an understanding of what message each sentence intends to convey.

2. *Preparation*: Divide students into four groups. Each group will be in charge of a type of sentence. If your classroom is already in teams, use the teams as your groups. If your class is very large, you could create a fifth group, and label them *sentences with interjections*.

3. *Challenge:* Your groups should come up with a cheer, phrase, or saying that defines a sentence type, as well as actions that visually depict what they are saying. Ask them to design a speech bubble from 9x17 construction paper and write in their saying. For example, sayings might be:

   Declarative: *I declare a statement* (point upwards with an index finger) *that ends in a period* (raise hands over your head into a giant circle, depicting a period).

   Interrogative: *Things that make you go hmmm . . .* (point to your chin and look puzzled).

Exclamatory: *Exclamatory shows EMOTION!* (make your hair stand on end).

Imperative: (in a strong commanding voice) *I, I, imperative, remember your period* (point to people in a commanding way).

1. Assign each group a corner of the room to hang their speech bubble poster from the ceiling.

2. As a large group, gather in the first corner, the declarative corner. The declarative group shares their chant and actions and the whole group practices it. This corner is now officially the declarative corner.

3. Repeat in the remaining corners.

4. To make it stick, return to Corner 1 and perform that chant again, then come back to Corner 2 and review it prior to moving on to Corners 3 and 4.

Results

The groups were 100% engaged and achieved 100% proficiency on the task. As time passed, I would point to a corner and they would all chant and do the motions correctly.

LESSON 7: FLOOR CALCULATOR

Issue: A colleague was having issues with his class remembering their multiplication facts. The typical drill and timed tests weren't working for many of his students.

U-Turn idea: Knowing many of his students were extremely kinesthetic, he decided to adapt the spelling hopscotch idea from *Green Light Classrooms*, where students practice their spelling words by *hopping them out* on a giant letter grid on the floor.

Translating the curriculum: In addition to his daily timed tests, he added kinesthetic practice using a giant floor calculator. His students would practice as a whole group, small group, or even at recess time!

Equipment

- Various colored 3 x 5 index cards—labeled with numbers 0–9, =, +, -, ×, and ÷ symbols
- Contact paper

Set up: In one corner, lay the cards out to depict a typical calculator and adhered them to the floor using contact paper.

Execution: Students stand around the calculator in a large circle. Give the first student a problem to solve, or let students choose one that they are having particular trouble remembering. Ask them to hop onto the calculator keys to solve the problem. So, if the first student chooses *9 x 6*, they hop on *9* then the *x* symbol then the *6*, then the *=* sign, and then finally the *5* and *4*, to get their answer of *54*. All the while, they chant what they are hopping on. If they get stuck, the other students may help by calling out the color of the card they need to hop to next.

Results

Students became more engaged and excited about solidifying their math facts. Their scores began to rise and they voluntarily practiced the particular problems they had most trouble with.

LESSON 8: FLOOR KEYBOARD

Issue: For many of my students, writing out their spelling words wasn't translating into good test scores. Some students were also struggling to remember where the letters go on a keyboard.

U-Turn idea: I decided to build a giant keyboard, so students could hop out their spelling words and review keyboard locations at the same time.

Translating the curriculum: In addition to our typical spelling practice, at least once a week, as a class, we surround the giant floor keyboard and practice hopping, or keyboarding our spelling words out in a kinesthetic way.

Equipment

- Squares of paper, about 4 x 4 inches in size, one color dedicated to consonants and one color dedicated to vowels
- Contact paper
- Stencils

Preparation

Ask your students to help you build the giant keyboard. Give each student a stencil letter and a 4 x 4 inch piece of paper. Using black permanent marker, ask them to trace and color in each letter of the alphabet. Lay all the letters on the floor in the keyboard configuration. Cut contact paper larger than the letter keys, and let your students adhere the letters to the floor. Make sure you leave plenty of hopping room.

Execution

Give each student a spelling word, or let them choose one that they are having difficulty remembering. When it's their turn, students shout out their word, and hop out the spelling, saying each letter as they land on it. As their word is complete, they shout out their word again to signal they are finished. This is the signal for the whole class to spell the word again out loud.

Results

The students begged to practice their spelling words and spelling scores rose! Especially for kinesthetic students, hopping out and visualizing the placement of the letter keys really increased their spelling skills. Also, during the test, they could peer at the keyboard and visualize how they jumped out the word, increasing their ability to remember how to spell those tricky words.

LESSON 9: WAX MUSEUM

Issue: My visual/kinesthetic learners were finding it hard to remember the definitions of important weekly vocabulary words. When discussing the words orally as the basal reader suggested, most were tuning me out and failing their weekly vocabulary tests.

U-Turn idea: To help students internalize their new vocabulary words, and *really* understand them, I decided they should **become** them. Thus the idea of creating a wax museum was born.

Translating the curriculum: Instead of orally reviewing our vocabulary, I challenged my students to become wax statues depicting the definition in a museum.

Equipment

- Vocabulary words on index cards
- Various props available (I keep a trunk full of hats, play swords, coats, dresses, etc.)

Procedure

- Place students in pairs or trios.
- Give each pair or trio a vocabulary word.
- Allow five to seven minutes for teams to determine how they will depict their word as still wax statues, as well as gather and create their props.
- In front of the class, groups take it in turn to become an exhibit. At the count of three, they strike their pose and hold it for a moment.
- Teams who are in the audience raise their hand to guess which word the current team is portraying. Take guesses until the correct one is given.
- Repeat until all the words have been covered.

Results

This activity always gets my students highly motivated! They often beg to practice their vocabulary in this fashion. As far as their understanding is concerned, ALL students are now achieving 100% on their tests, as well as storing the meanings in their long-term memories.

A TWIST on the Wax Museum: You could also ask students to create a short thirty-second skit portraying their words, or a thirty-second silent movie skit illustrating the definitions.

Note: Often when the last two or three groups are up performing, the audience has whittled down the words the final groups could possibly be portraying. Therefore, when I secretly give teams their words to portray, I may give two or more teams the same word, so as not to give it away.

LESSON 10: FACTOR NUMBER TILES

Issue: My verbal/kinesthetic learners often have a difficult time in math, because there isn't enough hands-on manipulation of the material in the older grades. This often leads to unmotivated and disconnected individuals.

U-Turn idea: Whenever possible, I try to make my math lessons as hands-on as possible. The trick is to see where students can move and manipulate the information instead of simply writing it down. For example, when learning about factors, students have to choose numbers that create the number. What better way than to provide number tiles for students to choose from and pull out of a number line?

Translating the curriculum: Previously, the students were supposed to write down a given number, say 36, and list all of its factors down on paper. Instead, my students now use number tiles to create a number grid, and from that number grid they easily pull the factors out of the line to visually show their factors.

Equipment

- 1 x 1 inch blank black-lined master grid (typically found with math series) copied on heavy colored card stock (two different colors if finding the GCF/LCF)
- Scissors
- Mailing envelopes (to store the manipulatives)
- Space to manipulate—clear off tables or give the option to use the floor

Procedure

1. *Preparation:* Prior to the lesson, maybe as a *sponge* activity, ask your students to number two different colors of grid card stock from 1–50 (or higher, depending on how many squares are on the grid paper) and cut each number box out and store in mailing envelopes or Ziploc bags for safe keeping.

2. *Discussion:* Begin the lesson by discussing numbers and their factors. Explain that *fact*-ors are simply the numbers or *facts* that make a particular number. Show an example on the board.

3. *Execution:* Give students a pile of number tiles in each color. One color is spread out in front of them in a nice sequential row; save the other color for later. Call out a number, say 8. The

students are then to pull out the factors of 8—1, 2, 4, 8 and place them at the top of their row. As the teacher, you can quickly and simply walk around to monitor and get a very quick visual of who has it and who doesn't. Then when it appears everyone has their factors pulled, ask them to shout them out:

Teacher: "What are the factors of 8?"

Students: "1, 2, 4, 8!"

Teacher: "Great, put them back into your pile. Let's do another."

Do this a few more times; make sure everyone has the idea.

4. Next, you need to find the greatest common and least common factor of two different numbers. Now it's time to pull out the other color tiles and make two rows of numbers.

5. At this point, ask your students to find the factors of 5 from your yellow cards, and the factors of 10 from your green cards and place them at the top of their piles. Now ask, "What are the common factors?" (List these on the board.) What is the *least* common? *Greatest* common? (Circle these on the board.)

6. Doing this a few times allows the students to manipulate, and the teacher to monitor very quickly.

7. At this point, you may want to assess, and this could be where students use paper and pencil to do a couple of exit problems to show what they know.

Results

Conducting math in this fashion increased engagement and understanding by 100%. No more passive students.

Review Techniques

When first learning new information, the mind essentially creates *rough drafts* of the concept. In rough draft form, new information often has only a very small pathway that is difficult to find. Therefore, we need to make sure learners will practice new concepts in various ways to create many memory pathways, so students will be able to retain and recall the material—hence the need for review.

The problem is that many students find traditional review techniques extremely boring. As a result, they tune out and fail to make any further connections with the material. The following review techniques will help you make the review process fun and engaging, making sure it achieves the objective of laying down stronger memory pathways.

Note: Many of these activities focus on vocabulary, since terminology is critical for state assessments!

REVIEW TECHNIQUE 1:
CLEAR PROJECTOR SHEET REVIEW

Material

- One-half to one clear projector sheet for each student
- 1 Vis-a-Vis or Expo marker for each student
- Sock or paper towel as an eraser
- Textbook

For many struggling students, going back into the text to find evidence to support their answers is extremely difficult and painful; therefore, they typically sit back and refuse to participate. Giving them a clear sheet and pen makes this extremely beneficial procedure seem easy and fun!

All students have to do is lay the clear sheet over the page in their text. When students have found the answer—or evidence that supports their answer—they simply underline it or circle it on the clear sheet. When complete, wipe off and do it again!

REVIEW TECHNIQUE 2: CONTAINERS,
CONTAINERS, CONTAINERS

Material

- Chinese containers (often found at dollar or craft stores)
- Various questions or problems cut apart
- White mini-boards or paper/pencil or chart paper
- Expo markers
- Calculators
- Answer keys

This style of review can easily be used for ANY subject matter. Begin by finding an old worksheet and cutting it apart. Put the problems or questions inside the containers and place one container on each table. Students randomly draw from the container, solve the problem, and check to see if they are correct. If it's a math problem, they can check themselves on the calculator. If the review is from another subject, make several answer keys, so students get up out of their seats to check themselves.

To keep your students accountable during this process, continually circulate and monitor progress by asking questions about how a student solved their problem, and what steps they took to get there.

Classroom Snapshot

I scour the dollar stores, craft stores, and Oriental Trading catalog for various and crazy containers. Over the years, I have used Easter eggs, Ziploc baggies, paper lunch bags, metal holiday minibuckets, empty plastic spice bottles, plastic test tubes, GIANT vitamin bottles, plastic storage minicontainers, and buckets of various sizes. For whatever reason, the sight of different containers got the kids excited about the review process, instead of the groans and moans that would resonate from my classroom. Today, I get cheers and curiosity is piqued when I pull out my array of containers—they don't seem to realize they are reviewing and learning!

REVIEW TECHNIQUE 3: SPELLING SCRAMBLE

Material

- Construction paper in four or five colors (depending on the number of table teams in your classroom)
- Cut each piece of construction paper into four equal squares; these will become letter tiles of about 3 x 5 inches
- Upbeat music like Michael Jackson's "ABC"

Set Up

- Ask your students to help make the letter tiles by placing each letter of the alphabet on each square, making sure the letters are very large and visible. Make at least two of each letter, and at least three of frequently used letters such as *M*, *N*, *L*, *P*, and all vowels.
- Laminate the cards for future use.

How to Play

Clear off tables. Hand each table team a different colored set of letter tiles to spread out over the table. At your cue, shout out a spelling word and turn on the music. Immediately, teams scramble to spell the word first and correctly using the spelling tiles. When they believe they have it correct, they shout, *SPELL-O!* Check them and give them a thumbs up . . . do this for ALL the groups. Once all the groups have spelled the word, spell it out loud together. If a team is having difficulty spelling the word, and the rest of the room is done, make sure you cheer that team on . . . *Yellow, Yellow, Yellow* until they get the word spelled correctly. *Never*, ever keep score, and *never*, ever allow a team to give up.

REVIEW TECHNIQUE 4: SELF-CHECK VELCRO YES/NO

Material

- Reading passages with multiple choice answers, laminated (I use excerpts from *Study Island*, as they correlate nicely with my state assessments.)
- Velcro dots
- Three-pronged folder for storage
- *Yes/No* squares or similar to the ones shown (about ½ inch square.)

Set Up

Cut and paste various passages and their multiple choice answers that reflect skills you have recently taught in class—such as main idea, character traits, or summarizing. Make sure you **bold** one of the answers (with a mix of correct and incorrect) prior to copying them off onto heavy card stock. Then laminate each page, three-hole punch it, and place it in a three-pronged folder for long use. Place a Velcro dot beside the four multiple choice questions as well as the matching Velcro dot to a *YES* or *NO* square.

How to Play

Tell your class that other students took the *Study Island test*. Partners are to read the passages together and decide if the student answered correctly (bolded answer) or if the bolded answer is incorrect. Once they have made their decision, they adhere their *Yes/No* square to the Velcro dot. If they believe the given answer is incorrect, they still adhere the *NO* dot, but they must also use an Expo or Vis-a-Vis marker to indicate the answer they think is correct. When a pair has completed their task, quickly check their answers, and ask them to go back and reexamine any incorrect choices. If there are still errors, this is a good time to give a minilesson on the strategy and get students to talk their way through their thinking.

REVIEW TECHNIQUE 5: MINI-ENVELOPES REVIEW

Material

- Nonfiction articles with completion questions
- The same number of mini coin-sized envelopes as you have questions
- Answers for the completion questions, typed out
- Completion questions cut into strips
- Partnering tool of some sort—for example, appointment people, matching fish

Set Up

Take the answers for the questions and type them up on a worksheet along with lines that follow. Take the completions questions that came with the text, cut them into strips, and put one strip in each envelope. Place the envelopes around the room.

How to Play

Students are paired up and asked to read the article. On completion, they are to scour the room for mini-envelopes. Once they find one, they open it up, read the question, and try to find an appropriate answer on their guide sheet. They write the question on their guide sheet—on the lines that follow the given answer—and place the question back into the envelope, put the envelope back where they found it, and move on to the next available envelope. They continue on in this fashion until they find all of the questions.

Giving your students the answers, and letting them find the corresponding questions, makes students really think about what they know. You'll see a lot of discussion and learning and you may find that slower learners struggle a little, which is why we recommend working in pairs.

Review Technique 6: 'Bendy' Vocabulary

Material

- Vocabulary lists
- Plastic bendable characters (the Mega bendable assortment from Oriental Trading, includes 100 various characters)
- Blank 8x10 copy paper
- Colored pencils/markers
- Vocabulary journals (optional)
- Sticky notes

Set Up

Let each student choose one bendable character and place a list of about seven to ten vocabulary words on the board, or specify which words from the word wall they can choose from.

How to Play

Each student secretly chooses a word from the vocabulary list. He or she then has five to seven minutes (be flexible with this) to place the bendable characters on their papers, and draw around the character creating a scene that defines the word choice. For example, a student choosing the word *rank*, meaning very smelly, might draw flies buzzing around the character, and people running away from him yelling, "Ewe, Yuck!," "Gross!" When the time is up, each student places a sticky note near the drawing. As music plays, students meander from one scene to the next, jotting on the sticky note what word they feel the picture is depicting. When everyone has had an opportunity to look at each creation, she returns to her seat to see how everyone did. As you set this up with your students, make the point that you WANT everyone to know what you are defining through your picture. It's NOT about stumping your fellow classmates, it's about defining your word through drawings well enough that people guess the definition. If time remains, allow each student to stand up and show their picture and clarify what they were drawing.

Review **TECHNIQUE** 7: "I'm Thinking of a Word"

(Adapted from *Classrooms That Work* by Patricia M. Cunningham and Richard L. Allington.)

Materials

- Sticky notes/index cards—one per student
- Word wall or vocabulary list

Secretly choose a word from your wall or list and jot it down on a sticky note. Give each student a sticky note on which they write the numbers 1–5. Give your students five clues as to the word you're thinking of. The first clue is always: *I'm thinking of a word, and it's a word wall/vocabulary list word.* After each clue, the students write down words they think fit your clues for each number. If the succeeding guesses match their original words, they still continue to write down that word for each clue. After the fifth clue, unveil your word!

Suggested CLUES

I'm thinking of a word. . .

- o . . . that is a word wall/vocabulary list word.
- o . . . that comes from the blue, green, yellow . . . section (if your words are color coded).
- o . . . that has _____ syllables.
- o . . . that has a prefix/suffix.
- o . . . that is a synonym/antonym to the word _____.
- o . . . that contains the word _____ in it.
- o . . . that is a noun, verb, adjective . . ..
- o . . . that begins/ends with the _____ sound.
- o . . . that would complete this sentence. . ..

Clearly this game works best if you have a word wall in your classroom, with words from different units written on different color paper. But a vocabulary list works just as well.

Appendix

Appointments—AM	
12:00	6:00
1:00	7:00
2:00	8:00
3:00	9:00
4:00	10:00
5:00	11:00

Appointments—PM

12:00	6:00
1:00	7:00
2:00	8:00
3:00	9:00
4:00	10:00
5:00	11:00

References

Allen, R. H. (2010). *High-impact teaching strategies for the 'XYZ' era of education.* Boston, MA: Pearson Education.

Boynton, M., & Boynton, C. (2005). *The educator's guide to preventing and solving discipline problems.* Alexandria, VA: Association for Supervision and Curriculum Development.

Buzan, T. (1996). *The mind map book: How to use radiant thinking to maximize your brain's untapped potential.* New York, NY: Penguin.

Cleveland, K. P. (2011). *Teaching boys who struggle in school: Strategies that turn underachievers into successful learners.* Alexandria, VA: Association for Supervision and Curriculum Development.

Cunningham, P. M., & Allington, R. L. (2003). *Classrooms that work: They can all read and write* (3rd ed.). Boston, MA: Allyn & Bacon.

Dodge, J. (2005). *Differentiation in action: A complete resource with research-supported strategies to help you plan and organize differentiated instruction—and achieve success with all learners.* New York, NY: Scholastic.

Fisher, D., & Frey, N. (2008). Releasing responsibility. *Educational Leadership, 66*(2), 32–36

Frey, N., Fisher, D., & Everlove, S. (2009). *Productive group work: How to engage students, build teamwork, and promote understanding.* Alexandria, VA: Association for Supervision and Curriculum Development.

Guskey, T. R., & Anderman, E. M. (2008). Students at bat. *Educational Leadership, 66*(3), 8–14.

Hattie, J. (2009). *Visible learning: A synthesis of over 800 meta-analyses relating to achievement.* New York, NY: Routledge.

Heck, T. (2009). *Duct tape teambuilding games—50 Fun activities to help your team stick together.* Asheville, NC: Life Coach, Inc.

Jensen, E. (2008). Brain-based learning: *The new paradigm of teaching* (2nd ed.). Thousand Oaks, CA: Corwin.

Johansen, J. P., Fields, H. L., & Manning, B. H. (2001, July 3). The affective component of pain in rodents: Direct evidence for a contribution of the anterior cingulate cortex. *Proceedings of the National Academy of Sciences, USA 98*(14), 8077–8082. doi:10.1073/pnas.141218998. Retrieved from http://emotion.caltech.edu/dropbox/bil33/files/%20Johansen%20et%20al.pdf

Lyman, F. (1981). The responsive classroom discussion: The inclusion of all students. In A. S. Anderson (Ed.), *Mainstreaming Digest* (pp. 109–113). College Park: University of Maryland Press.

Marzano, R. J. (2007). The art and science of teaching: A comprehensive framework for effective instruction. Alexandria, VA: Association for Supervision and Curriculum Development.

Marzano, R. J., & Pickering, D. J., (2011). *The highly engaged classroom.* Bloomington, IN: Marzano Research Laboratory.

Marzano, R. J., Pickering, D. J., & Pollock, J. E. (2001). *Classroom instruction that works: Research-based strategies for increasing student achievement.* Alexandria, VA: Association for Supervision and Curriculum Development.

Ritchhart, R., & Perkins, D. (2008). Making thinking visible. *Educational Leadership, 65*(5), 57–61.

Sapolsky, R. M. (2004). *Why zebras don't get ulcers* (3rd ed.). New York, NY: Henry Holt.

Sousa, D., & Tomlinson, C. (2011). *Differentiation and the brain: How neuroscience supports the learner-friendly classroom.* Bloomington, IN: Solution Tree Press.

Swartz, R. (2008). Energizing learning. *Educational Leadership, 65*(5), 26–31.

Tate, M. (2003). *Worksheets don't grow dendrites: 20 instructional strategies that engage the brain.* Thousand Oaks, CA: Corwin.

Tomlinson, C. A. (2008). Giving students ownership of learning. *Educational Leadership, 66*(3), 26–30.

Van Praag, H., Kempermann, G., & Gage, F. H. (1999). Running increases cell proliferation and neurogenesis in the adult mouse dendate gyrus. *Nature Neuroscience, 2,* 266–270. doi: 10.1038/6368

Wolk, S. (2008). Joy in school. *Educational Leadership, 66*(1), 8–14.

Zapf, S. (2008). Reaching the fragile student. *Educational Leadership, 66*(1), 67–70.

Index

CORWIN

A SAGE Company

The Corwin logo—a raven striding across an open book—represents the union of courage and learning. Corwin is committed to improving education for all learners by publishing books and other professional development resources for those serving the field of PreK–12 education. By providing practical, hands-on materials, Corwin continues to carry out the promise of its motto: **"Helping Educators Do Their Work Better."**